HAMMERIN'
HANK GREENBERG

HAMMERIN' HANK GREENBERG

Baseball Pioneer

Shelley Sommer

CALKINS CREEK

HONESDALE, PENNSYLVANIA

ISBN: 978-1-59078-452-5

Library of Congress Control Number: 2010929519

Front jacket and page 3: Hank Greenberg at bat in the mid-1930s.
Back jacket: Hank Greenberg and the Detroit Tigers in 1935, the year they won the World Series.

CALKINS CREEK
An Imprint of Boyds Mills Press, Inc.
815 Church Street
Honesdale, Pennsylvania 18431

10 9 8 7 6 5 4 3 2 1

*For Tom and Bob, who taught me the joy of baseball,
and for my father, Robert Kurtz, who learned along with me*

ACKNOWLEDGMENTS

This book would not have been written without the support and guidance of Esther Newberg, Carolyn P. Yoder, Jill Goodman, Juanita Galuska, and Paul Park; Donna Milani Luther and all of my other colleagues at Inly School; Joanne Kaplan; Gabriel Schecter and John Horne at the National Baseball Hall of Fame; and Andrew Gutelle. I also want to thank Stephen Greenberg, Hank's son, for reviewing the manuscript, and Susan Bloom, without whom this book would not exist. Finally, I am grateful for the good cheer supplied by my family in Ohio and New Mexico.

CONTENTS

Hammerin' Hank Greenberg

1

THE JEWISH SUPERSTAR

THE STANDS AT PITTSBURGH'S FORBES FIELD were packed on May 15, 1947, as the Pirates opened a three-game series against the visiting Brooklyn Dodgers. The Dodgers had played at Forbes Field dozens of times in past seasons, but on this day something in the air was different. Some fans were there to cheer for the hometown team, but most had come to see the new member of the Brooklyn Dodgers—Jackie Robinson. Some were merely curious and excited to watch him. But others were angry at seeing a black man take the field as a major league player. That included several members of the Pittsburgh Pirates. "Hey, coal mine, hey you black coal mine, we're going to get you! You ain't gonna play no baseball," some of them shouted.

One player who was not angry was the Pirates' first baseman, Hank Greenberg.

"I forgot to ask you if you were hurt in that play," Hank Greenberg said to Jackie Robinson after the two collided during a routine play at first base. "Stick in there. You're doing fine. Keep your chin up," Greenberg told Robinson. Hank Greenberg was one of the few people who understood what Robinson was going through.

But Hank Greenberg was Jewish, not black. Now in the last of his thirteen years in the major leagues, Greenberg had survived prejudice and insults that were different from Robinson's. He knew what the young player was up against. And Robinson appreciated Greenberg's gesture. "Class tells. It sticks out all over Mr. Greenberg," Robinson said later.

Fourteen years before Robinson joined the Brooklyn Dodgers, Greenberg broke a different kind of barrier. As America's first Jewish baseball star, he became used to hearing people yell "Kike" and "Jew bastard" from the stands.

Jewish baseball players had made it to the big leagues before Greenberg, but Greenberg became a superstar at a time when religious bigotry was common. He was the child of Romanian immigrants, and like many first-generation Americans, he understood that sports was one way to fit in. And so, young Hank played. He played on the streets of the Bronx in New York City even though his parents thought it was a waste of time. They wanted him to succeed—to graduate from college and find a respectable and secure profession.

From the beginning, Greenberg was a better player than the other neighborhood kids. It wasn't long before adults, including coaches and scouts from major league baseball teams, recognized his talent. Right after Hank graduated from high school, Pat McDonald, a local policeman who had won a gold medal in the shot put in the 1912 Olympics, said to him, "Young man, I just came from watching the Yankees play, and, by God, you hit a ball better than Lou Gehrig."

Hank Greenberg was six foot three by the time he was thirteen years old, a fact that sometimes caused him embarrassment. "I began to think I was a freak," he said. His height, though, combined with his physical strength, made him the perfect first baseman, the position he played for the Detroit Tigers for seven years, before moving to left field. Traditionally, players at first base are some of the taller guys on the team. Their long reach allows them to snare balls thrown from infielders before the runner can reach

first base. But although Greenberg played in four World Series, was selected to five All-Star teams, was the American League's Most Valuable Player two times, and came within two home runs of Babe Ruth's single-season home run record in 1938, he did all of it while always being jeered from the sidelines and referred to as the "Jewish ballplayer."

Before joining the Dodgers, Jackie Robinson played shortstop for the Kansas City Monarchs, a Negro League team.

Being Jewish in the 1930s was not like being black. Hank was taller than most of his teammates, but otherwise his difference was not noticeable. "In the case of Jackie Robinson, Jackie had no place to go after a ball game and Greenberg could go anyplace in the world. Greenberg had to bear that terrible burden on the field, Jackie had to bear it all his life," said one of Greenberg's teammates, Birdie Tebbetts. But still, Tebbetts recalled, "There was nobody in the history of the game who took more abuse than Greenberg, unless it was Jackie Robinson."

In 1933, the year Hank Greenberg joined the Detroit Tigers, the country was in the midst of an economic depression. People wanted to know what was going on, and it was radio that kept them up-to-date on news and entertainment. Radio was also used by some to attack politicians and

The 1945 Detroit Tigers. Hank is seated in the second row from the bottom, fourth from the right.

spread fear. On Saturdays, millions of people tuned in to Father Charles Coughlin, the "Radio Priest," who delivered messages rooted in prejudice and anti-Semitism. "Must the entire world go to war for 600,000 Jews in Germany?" he asked in 1939, the beginning of World War II. Coughlin's *Golden Hour of the Little Flower* was broadcast from Detroit, the city where Hank Greenberg lived and played.

Many American Jews like Greenberg were finding success in the United States, but the experience of German Jews was starkly different. With the appointment of Adolf Hitler as Germany's chancellor in 1933, Jews began to find their rights harshly limited. In 1936, three years into Hank Greenberg's baseball career, Germany hosted the Summer Olympic Games, referred to as the "Nazi Olympics" because Hitler used the games to promote the Nazi Party's belief in the superiority of the "Aryan race." The 1936 Olympics were most notable, however, for the performance of a black American track star, Jesse Owens.

During that same year, another sports event caught the attention of people on both sides of the Atlantic Ocean. This one took place in the boxing ring. Joe Louis, a black boxer, was knocked out in a match in New York against the German fighter Max Schmeling. Schmeling's victory over the previously undefeated Louis was trumpeted by Nazi officials as a symbol of Germany's strength. In fact, one Nazi newspaper reported, "Schmeling's victory was not only sport. It was a question of prestige for our race." Two years later, Louis defeated Schmeling in the first round.

The baseball diamond, the running track, and the boxing ring were just three of the places where racial and ethnic tensions of the 1930s were on display. But, throughout it all, Hank Greenberg, a big man in many ways, stood tall.

Hank Greenberg's first home in Greenwich Village, New York City. Greenberg, his parents, and older brother and sister lived on the second floor until Hank was a year old, when they moved to a different apartment in the same neighborhood.

2

A NEW YORK BOYHOOD

FROM THE WINDOW OF THEIR THREE-STORY house in the Bronx, David and Sarah Greenberg could watch their son Hank become an American.

Hank, the third of their four children, could usually be found playing baseball in the streets, just like all of the other boys in the neighborhood. And like other adults in the neighborhood, Hank's parents were Yiddish-speaking Jewish immigrants who did not understand their son's fascination with baseball. To them, it was a waste of time. But for Hank and other kids growing up in New York City at the beginning of the twentieth century, baseball was the best way to fit in. It made them less foreign and more American. Hank played it, he remembered later, "anytime there was less than a foot of snow."

Like many Jewish immigrants in the late 1800s, David and Sarah Greenberg had come to America from a small Romanian town. They wanted to live in a place where they were free to express their religious beliefs and make a life for themselves based on hard work and equal opportunity. Like

New York City's famous Fifth Avenue in 1913.

many newcomers, David and Sarah Greenberg gave up far more than their native land. They had to learn a new language and leave family and friends behind, unsure if they would ever see them again. But they also had dreams for their children's future.

Henry Benjamin Greenberg was born on New Year's Day, 1911. As one of thousands of babies born to newly arrived immigrant parents, he became part of a generation that dramatically changed New York City as well as the United States.

Four years before Hank was born, more people arrived in New York City from Europe than ever before—1,200,000 people in all. By the mid-1900s, New York was the "largest Jewish city in the world, the largest Irish city, and it contained more Italians than Rome." New York's streets were chock-full with people speaking different languages but sharing many of the same dreams.

All day long one could hear the sounds of trolley cars going up and down the streets, and construction crews building the New York subway system and America's first skyscrapers. Both were monuments to growth and progress—as well as practical solutions to New York's overcrowding. New York City, much of it set on an island, needed to build *over* and *under* the streets, rather than spreading out.

One immigrant, upon arriving in New York City and seeing the Statue of Liberty and the tall buildings, said, "I thought I was in Heaven ... Was this a city on earth or a city in heaven?"

The construction of new buildings and a subway system created jobs for the immigrants, although they were low paying and often dangerous. Many immigrants, including Hank's father, worked in factories. But David Greenberg was a factory owner. Hank's childhood was more comfortable than those of many immigrant children. Sarah, his mother, was able to stay home and care for him and his brothers and sister. Hank recalled that it was important to his parents that their children ate good meals. "He kept the house well supplied with the basic foods," Hank said about his father. "He thought if he fed his kids well they would be healthy and grow up strong."

In the early 1900s, New York City was the center of the American clothing industry. The workers in David Greenberg's factory shrunk fabric so it could be used to make suits. More people were buying ready-made clothes than ever before, and there was a growing number of immigrants willing to work for low wages, making clothes less expensive and more plentiful.

Until Hank was six or seven years old, the family lived in Greenwich Village at the southern end of Manhattan, which was home to many immigrant families. "A small group of Jewish families lived in this same apartment building," Hank remembered. "We all spoke the same language, and as a result we lived close to each other. This was common among immigrants who came from Europe."

The children living in the apartments used the street as their playground. It was here that Hank learned to play stickball, a sport like baseball. Manhole covers served as bases, and a strike zone could be drawn with chalk on the side of a building. All kids needed were a ball and a broomstick or mop handle for a bat. Using hard balls in crowded city streets led to a lot of broken windows and some angry neighbors!

But Hank remembered another "sport" that was not fun. In neighborhoods where each block was home to a different ethnic group, tensions and

The street served as a ballpark for kids in New York City during the early part of the twentieth century. Note the laundry hanging above them.

frustrations were acted out. "Kids down in the Village thought the national pastime was beating up kids of other nationalities," Hank said later.

Hank's parents believed that their neighborhood was getting rough, and so like many Jewish families, they decided to move north to the Bronx. Living in the Bronx was like stepping back in time. Although most people traveled around the city by the new subway system or one of the many trolley cars, it was still common to see a horse and wagon in the Bronx. For Hank, the move was "a turning point." His family's neighborhood, Crotona Park, had plenty of open space to play, and his new school, Public School 44, had baseball and basketball teams.

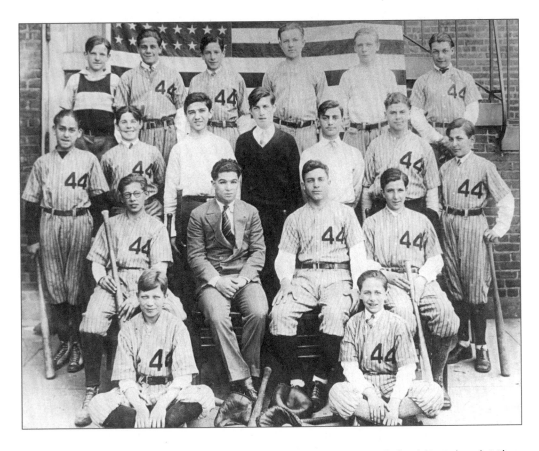

Many of the graduating students from Farragut Junior High (Public School 44) wore their baseball uniforms in 1926. Greenberg is standing in the back row, third from the left.

After attending elementary school and junior high at Public School 44 —where, according to Hank, sports were always on his mind—he, his older brother and sister, Ben and Lillian, and his younger brother, Joe, moved on to James Monroe High School, a forty-minute walk from their house. He played on the school's baseball, basketball, and soccer teams and even tried track and football "to prove that I wasn't a coward," he said.

By the time Hank was thirteen years old, he was six feet three inches tall and remembered feeling "awkward." "At school, I'd squeeze behind one of those tiny desks, and if I had to go to the blackboard it would be the event of the day … Everybody always teased me. 'How's the air up there?' I heard that a dozen times a day … Sports was my escape from all that." It did not take long for Hank, because of his height and abilities, to become known as a talented athlete.

Hank recalled later that he played baseball for "hours on end." "On weekdays after school, I'd rush to the park with my glove, bat and ball and come home only after it got dark. Weekends were completely devoted to the old field, and instead of coming home for lunch, I'd fill my pockets with fruit and candy and stay down at the ballpark all day … the days weren't long enough …" "My father used to holler at me that I would never make anything of myself, but when the next day came, I was back playing baseball."

To David and Sarah Greenberg, their son's passion for a game they knew little about was confusing. They had moved to a new country, given up everything familiar, and wanted their children to succeed in "mainstream America." Although his parents couldn't see it, Hank was making a success of himself in America's national pastime.

Hank played baseball in the same city as three major league teams, but he wasn't aware of them until he was fourteen years old. "It was like another world," he said. When he did learn about the New York Giants, the Brooklyn Dodgers, and the New York Yankees, he went with the winners—and became a Giants fan.

Although Hank's family had money by 1920s standards, going to a major league game was not something they even considered. "Travel was restricted to subway rides," he remembered. "No one had a nickel to get on the subway, let alone the money to buy a ticket to a ball game."

But when Hank was fourteen, his dad came up with the extra money to take his son to a Sunday doubleheader between the Giants and the Phillies. The Giants played in Manhattan at the Polo Grounds, a place named for a different sport. Polo had not been played on the site since the late 1800s, but the name stuck. "I still remember," Hank recalled later, "that Frankie Frisch, the Fordham Flash, a New York boy, got seven hits for the Giants double-header."

SEASON OF 1887.

HOME GAMES OF THE NEW YORK BALL CLUB FOR THE LEAGUE CHAMPIONSHIP.

April 28, 29,	with Philadelphia.	June 9, 10, 11,	with Washington.	Aug. 22, 28,	with Pittsburg.	
May 5, 6, 7,	" Boston.	" 18, 14, 15,	" Philadelphia.	" 25, 26, 27,	" Chicago.	
" 9, 10, 11,	" Washington.	July 7, 8, 9,	" Detroit.	" 29, 30, 31,	" Indianapolis.	
" 14,	" Philadelphia.	" 11, 12, 13,	" Pittsburg.	Sept. 1, 2, 3,	" Detroit.	
" 16, 17, 18,	" Indianapolis.	" 15, 16, 18,	" Chicago.	" 5, 6, 7,	" Washington.	
" 20, 21, 23, 24,	" Pittsburg.	" 19, 20, 21,	" Indianapolis.	" 26, 27, 28,	" Boston.	
" 26, 27, 28,	" Detroit.	" 23, 25, 26,	" Boston.	Oct. 5, 6, 6,	" Philadelphia.	
" 30 A M & P M 31	" Chicago.					

Between 1883 and 1957, the New York Giants played at the Polo Grounds, named for the sport for which it was first designed. The original polo stadium was built in 1876. Four years later, it was being used for baseball games. Four different stadiums built between 1876 and 1957 were all referred to as the Polo Grounds.

After that, Hank was hooked on the team. He followed the Giants on an electric scoreboard in a neighborhood store window. "The lights would flash when a man would get on base, and they would have two line-ups printed on the side and a little bulb to indicate who was at bat. We'd stand out on the street for hours watching the game with hundreds of other people."

Besides baseball, Hank and his friends enjoyed going to the movies. The movies were silent but were often accompanied by a piano player, or sometimes a small orchestra would play along with the action on the screen. "In those days," one Bronx resident remembered, "to go to a movie theater meant more than seeing a show. In a sense it was going to a world that seemed forbidden, a world of fantasy and of fabulous wealth."

But even the movies could not distract Hank from baseball. He did his schoolwork because it was what his parents expected, and he was a better-than-average student. He participated in the Jewish traditions, including family holiday gatherings and a celebration of his bar mitzvah when he was

After playing for the New York Giants for nine seasons, Frankie Frisch was traded to the Cardinals, where he played between 1928 and 1937 and was a standout second baseman.

thirteen. But he was also asking every kid in Crotona Park to pitch balls to him. "You do this all day long, every day, day after day, and sooner or later you're bound to get pretty good."

Hank's parents, of course, continued to hope that their son would pursue a college education and then a suitable career, but Hank was torn between his parents' expectations and opportunities his parents could not have dreamed possible. Although baseball remained his first love, he also excelled at basketball. "In basketball, I was much taller than the rest of the players, and I was a pretty physical player. I weighed about 215 or 220 pounds at that time … all skin and bones, but I was pretty strong." After being named to the all-scholastic basketball team during his senior year, Hank was offered a basketball scholarship to New York University. He was such a successful high-school athlete that under his yearbook picture are the words "Look up the record."

He was on his way.

Hank Greenberg in his James Monroe High School basketball uniform, 1929.

Detroit, Michigan (shown here in 1929), was hit hard by the stock market crash. By 1932, the city had a 43 percent unemployment rate.

3

LEARNING TO BE A TIGER

A BAD DAY FOR ONE OF HIS HIGH-SCHOOL teammates turned out to be a good day for Hank. In 1928, Paul Krichell, a scout for the New York Yankees, came to one of Hank's baseball games to watch the pitcher. Hank, in his final year of high school, played first base regularly. He planned to enroll at New York University in the fall. But Krichell quickly lost interest in the pitcher and started focusing his attention on the first baseman. Krichell became a regular at Hank's games. "Wherever I played, there was Mr. Krichell, watching me and taking notes," he said.

During the summer before starting college, Hank was on a semiprofessional baseball team, the Bay Parkways, a Brooklyn-based team. In the late 1920s, semipro teams were neighborhood-based and made up of players like Hank and former professionals. Some players were paid, and others, including Hank, were not. Hank didn't hit very well in his first few games, but it wasn't long before that changed. One Sunday, after he hit three home runs in a doubleheader, Hank decided to talk to George Lippe, the manager of the Bay Parkways, about the possibility of being paid. "I am an amateur," Hank said. "But, look, Mr. Lippe, it took me two hours to get out here and it's going to take me that long to get home. I won't be home until about eleven tonight, and I left home at eight in the morning. Besides, I had a pretty good day. I expect to get paid, or I'm not coming back." Lippe gave Hank five dollars and promised him ten dollars to play in an upcoming doubleheader. Hank didn't quit. "Ten dollars for a kid just out of high school was pretty good," he said.

After twenty-one games with the Bay Parkways, Hank was hitting .454 and attracting the attention of scouts for other semipro—and professional—teams. A scout for the Detroit Tigers, Jean Dubuc, arranged for Hank to play on a semipro team in East Douglas, Massachusetts.

Following a good season in East Douglas, Hank returned home to New York, where he received another visit from Paul Krichell. The Yankees, Krichell told him, were looking for a Jewish player to appeal to the team's many Jewish fans, and Greenberg was a good prospect.

"How'd you like to play for the Yankees?" Ed Barrow, the secretary-business manager of the Yankees, asked Hank. Of course, he was interested—until he went to Yankee Stadium

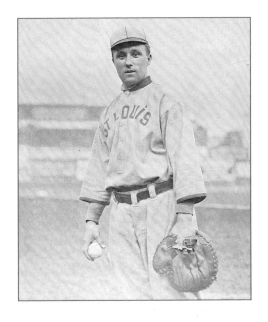

Paul Krichell was the Yankees' head scout for thirty-seven years. Before that, he played two seasons with the St. Louis Browns. His first game was in 1911, the year Greenberg was born.

and watched Lou Gehrig at first base. Hank was, as he put it, "in awe" of the Yankees' star. "His shoulders were a yard wide and his legs looked like mighty oak trees. I'd never seen such sheer brute strength," Hank recalled. Although Krichell thought Gehrig's best playing years might be behind him, Hank did not agree. "I had a look at Lou Gehrig, and said no thank you."

It took some time for the Yankees to make Hank an offer, but when they did, he turned it down. Krichell tried to persuade his young prospect to reconsider. He pointed out that Gehrig's batting average had slipped (in 1929), but his words fell on deaf ears. Hank said later that Krichell could not have changed his mind. After watching Gehrig, Hank knew that first base for the Yankees was already taken.

But the Yankees were not the only major league baseball team interested in the big first baseman. Jean Dubuc, on behalf of the American League Detroit Tigers, offered Hank six thousand dollars in cash when he signed a contract and another three thousand dollars after he finished college and was ready to move to Detroit. Hank's father was amazed that his son was offered so much money to play baseball. His parents encouraged him to accept the deal. "They figured that if the Detroit people thought enough of me to give me $9,000 before I even played a game for them, I must have some ability."

Hank knew very little about Detroit when he signed with the Tigers. He knew about Ty Cobb, of course, and some of the other great players in Tiger history but not very much about the city. He was eager to begin his career with the team—too eager to wait for four years. In January, after spending one semester at New York University, when newspapers were full of stories about the upcoming baseball season, he left college. "Pop," he said to his father, "I've got to go down there [to spring training in Florida]. I've got to play."

Greenberg started with Detroit's Triple A organization, a league one step below the majors, but it was not an easy time for the young prospect. He began his major league career at the Tigers' training camp in Tampa, Florida, and the nineteen-year-old Greenberg felt overwhelmed. "I just sat around the clubhouse with my eyes wide open and my mouth shut

Ty Cobb (left) had a lifetime batting average of .367. He is shown here around 1913 with Cleveland Naps (later called the Cleveland Indians) player Joe Jackson, considered to be one of the best hitters in baseball.

and just listened to them and watched them. They were all grown men, well groomed and well dressed … I guess most of them didn't understand why I was there." To make matters worse, the other players "did not want to mingle." Prospects like Hank moved around regularly between the various minor league and semipro teams—all of them hoping for a permanent position on a major league team. As one of the boys in the clubhouse explained to Hank, many of the players saw their teammates as competition. Baseball teams have a limited number of spots and so the closer a player gets to the big leagues, the fiercer the competition becomes.

After watching Greenberg strike out regularly, Frank Navin, the owner of the Tigers, decided that the rookie should get some experience on the Tigers' less competitive A team in Hartford, Connecticut. Every major league organization has several minor league teams, or farm clubs, where young players can develop. Hank realized that Navin was doing what he thought was best, and Hank agreed to play in Hartford.

"Playing semipro ball three times a week was quite different from playing every day against professional ballplayers," Hank remembered. "I tried hard but I was a big, awkward giraffe at first base. I missed pop flies over my head. I would get my feet tangled on ground balls." Hank knew the team's management wanted to give him an opportunity to improve. After all, the Tigers had invested nine thousand dollars in him. He was paid more than any other player on the team, and yet he continued to strike out routinely. Greenberg's time in Hartford was even more challenging because he was often compared with Lou Gehrig—who also started his professional career on the same Hartford team. "Because I was a first baseman from New York, the fans there anticipated that I would play as well as Lou did. Unfortunately, I was very green and inexperienced. I was eager, but still

Frank Navin (standing, far left) was the principal owner of the Detroit Tigers between 1909 and 1935. He is pictured here in 1914 with other American League team presidents and owners attending a baseball executives meeting. Standing next to Navin: Benjamin Minor (Washington Senators) and Frank Farrell (New York Yankees). Sitting (left to right): Charles Comiskey (Chicago White Sox), Ban Johnson (American League president), and Joseph Lannin (Boston Red Sox).

that inexperience was terribly important … And I felt all the pressure."

Greenberg described the twelve games he played in Hartford as "a total bust." He struck out thirteen times in a row. The Detroit management decided to reassign Hank to another of its farm clubs, this one in Raleigh, North Carolina.

In Raleigh, Hank was a curiosity—a Jewish kid from the Bronx. "My teammates were a bunch of farm boys and I was a big, ungainly kid from the city," Hank remembered. "One day I was standing on the field when I became aware of a teammate walking slowly around me, staring.

"'What're you looking at?' I asked.

"'Nothing,' he said. 'I've never seen a Jew before. I'm just looking …' I let him keep looking for awhile, and then I said, 'See anything interesting?'

"'I don't understand it,' he said. 'You look just like anybody else.'"

Hank may have looked like everyone else, but it was time for him to prove that he was a better baseball player than his minor league teammates. He continued his slump in Raleigh, until one day, a pitcher made a remark that jarred Greenberg. According to Greenberg, the pitcher "hollered the full length of the bus, 'Look at you, you big bum! What a slugger you are! I'm hitting .155 and you're slugging along at a terrific pace of .151!' That really made me sore, and that day I got four for four."

Hank began going to the park early—just as he had in Crotona Park— to practice. "It wasn't hard to talk some of the other guys into doing the same thing. What else was there to do in most of those minor league towns besides play ball?" he said.

By the end of the 1930 season, his slump was over, and the Tigers management invited him to travel with the major league team for the last three weeks of the season. Because the Tigers were in fifth place, Greenberg assumed he would get to play, but most of his time was spent sitting on the bench. Finally, on September 14, 1930, he stepped up to the plate for his first official "at bat" for the majors, and it was against the New York Yankees. Babe Ruth was in the Yankees lineup that day, and so was Gehrig, who hit

.379 that season. Hank's debut was not impressive. "I was as good as out before I ever reached the plate … I was scared to death," he remembered. "I popped up to [Yankees' second baseman] Tony Lazzeri, and I figured that everybody in the stands thought I was a gawky freak."

At the end of the season, he went home to New York. Although he was a "semicelebrity" in his Bronx neighborhood, there were still some people who doubted he was really a paid athlete. While driving in Manhattan, Hank ran a red light. The police officer looked at Hank's driver's license and then asked him about his work. Now, Hank was not only tall, but he was stronger and more confident, and he told the policeman that he was a professional baseball player. The officer "looked at my driver's license again and burst out laughing. 'And who in the hell ever heard of a professional ballplayer named Greenberg?' he said." Hank said later that the "incident was the fitting end to my first professional season."

The police officer's reaction to Hank was typical for the 1930s. There were Jewish boxers who had earned reputations in the ring. Abe Attell, who was the World Featherweight Champion in 1903 and 1904 and between 1906 and 1912, was nicknamed "The Little Hebrew." And there was Abe Goldstein, the 1924 World Bantamweight Champion. But there were few Jewish athletes attracting attention on the baseball diamond. In 1935, a Jewish newspaper columnist wrote: "As a rule, Jewish boys are smaller than kids who spring from other races. The Jewish boy was pushed aside on the playground diamond by the bigger youth with an Irish, German or Scandinavian name … For centuries, the Jew, in his individual business, had to fight against heavy odds for his success. It sharpened his wit and made him quick with his hands. Therefore, he became an individualist in sport, a skillful boxer and ring strategist, but he did not have the background to stand out in a sport which is so essentially a team game as baseball."

After spending the summer in New York, Hank was assigned to another Tigers farm team, this one in Beaumont, Texas. Frank Navin confirmed in a letter that the brief time Hank spent in Detroit was designed to introduce him to the major league atmosphere. Navin also let Hank know that they decided to send him to Beaumont because the young player needed more experience before a permanent move to the major leagues could be discussed. "If you can make the grade at Beaumont you can consider you are progressing very rapidly," Navin wrote.

Hank's stay in Beaumont was short. The team already had a first baseman, who, Hank acknowledged, was a better player. Hank, now twenty years old, was reassigned to Evansville, Indiana. He played well in Evansville, ending the season at .318. "All my hard work and all the time I spent working on my fielding and taking batting practice started to pay off," he said.

Hank spent the 1932 season back in Beaumont, Texas, where it was, in his words, "hot as blazes." "Someone came up with the idea of having red uniforms," he said. "So we sweated in these heavy, coarse horse blankets for uniforms while playing in temperatures of a hundred degrees." Hank had his best minor league season. He hit 39 homes runs, drove in 131 runs, and was chosen as the Texas

People lining up for food in New York City. Bread lines like this one were common sights during the Great Depression.

League's most valuable player. After that, Frank Navin wrote Hank a letter asking him to join the Tigers at spring training for the 1933 season.

When Hank began his major league career that year, America was in the fourth year of the Great Depression. Four years earlier, in October of 1929, the United States stock market crash caused many Americans to lose their jobs, businesses, and homes. While Hank's job was becoming more secure, the same could not be said for most Americans.

Young and old wait near Navin Field for tickets to the 1935 World Series between the Tigers and the Chicago Cubs.

4

HARD TIMES IN DETROIT

DETROIT WAS ESPECIALLY HARD HIT BY THE Great Depression. Known as Motor City, it was home to America's three biggest car manufacturers: Ford, General Motors, and Chrysler. But with so many people out of work, there was little need for shiny new cars coming off the assembly lines.

People were looking for work, waiting in front of factory gates, hoping to make enough money to buy dinner for their families. Although a ticket to a Detroit Tigers game was only one dollar—or fifty cents for the bleachers—it was still something that most families could not afford. In 1933, Greenberg's first full season, only 321,000 people went to a Tigers game in downtown Detroit.

During the mid-1930s, seeing the game in person was practically the only way to follow baseball. Although radios could be found in most living rooms, only the World Series games were given play-by-play coverage. Newspapers included baseball scores, but unless you purchased a late edition on your way home from work or walked by an electronic scoreboard in a store window, you waited until the next day to find out if your favorite team won or lost.

For many fans, a live game was a once-in-a-lifetime experience. The men, often arriving in the late innings after leaving work, wore suits and hats. Unemployed men took breaks from the job search, women wore dresses and heels, and boys hawked scorecards, popcorn, and peanuts.

One fan wrote that "Attending a game meant a lot, to adults as well as to a boy, because it was the only way you could encounter athletes and watch what they did. There was no television, no instant replay, no evening highlights … Seeing the players in action on the field, always at a little distance, gave them a heroic tinge." A teammate of Greenberg's, Charlie Gehringer, said, "Everybody dressed like they were going to the theater or maybe to church."

During the years when Frank Navin and then Walter Briggs owned the Tigers, ballpark employees dressed in uniforms. The Tigers' first two stadiums—Navin Field (1912–1938) and Briggs Stadium (1938–1960)—were named for the team's owners.

The players, wearing flat baseball caps and gloves a little bit larger than their hands, seemed bigger than life.

If people were lucky enough to go to the game on Labor Day, they could witness the tradition of the men in the stands "sailing their hats" onto the field when the Tigers made their first good play. Ty Cobb, Detroit's center fielder between 1905 and 1926, asked the batboys and groundskeepers to collect the hats so that the donkeys on his Georgia farm could wear them as protection from the sun.

Twenty-two-year-old Greenberg, like all of his teammates, knew that Tigers fans making the trip downtown to Navin Field were looking for a chance to escape their worries, if only for a few hours. "I knew things were tough on the outside," Greenberg said, "but I was young and trying to make my own way in life. We all knew what was going on, but we couldn't do anything about it. We just did our own jobs the best way we knew how. We knew that everyone was behind us and that was a good feeling."

The players, too, felt the effect of hard times. Professional baseball was not a particularly high-paying job. In his first year with the Tigers, Greenberg collected the three-thousand-dollar bonus guaranteed by his original contract. With that, he paid for the hotel room where he lived, meals, and other expenses. "Most everyone was broke. We used to sit around in the hotel lobby waiting for someone to drop a newspaper." He didn't live in Detroit's most luxurious hotel either, but that didn't matter to a young baseball player trying to get a start. Greenberg remembered that the players would look for cheap hotels. "When I first came to Detroit," he said, "I stayed at the Wolverine Hotel, for eight bucks a week. They gave you a room with a bed but no closets. It was no problem … since we took most of our showers at the ballpark, our bathrooms in the hotel became our closets."

By 1933, the Depression had already put one Detroit sports team out of business. The Detroit Stars, the city's Negro League team, just couldn't make enough money to survive. Many blacks had left the South and moved

Charlie Gehringer is considered to be one of the greatest second basemen of all times. His entire playing career—nineteen years—was with the Detroit Tigers.

to Detroit during the 1920s to work in the new automobile industry, but when the factories began laying people off, it was the end of the Stars. The players, many of whom worked in the automobile factories themselves, couldn't afford to stay in Detroit, and their fans couldn't afford to support their team.

Like his teammates, Greenberg tried to give Detroit's fans their hard-earned money's worth. But the first challenge Greenberg faced in Detroit was getting into the lineup. Although he went there expecting to be the Tigers' first baseman, the position was not immediately available. Harry Davis, a player selected by Tigers manager Bucky Harris, was already at first base, and Greenberg began the 1933 spring training season playing third base. "I put on a fielder's glove and worked like a dog, but I was awkward," said Greenberg. "I had never used anything but a first baseman's mitt and I didn't even know how to work the fingers on a regular glove." Early reviews were not promising. One Detroit sportswriter described Greenberg as a "big sweaty kid who looked pretty grotesque." It wasn't long before Greenberg was out of the lineup.

Still sitting on the bench by opening day in Detroit, he decided to visit Frank Navin. But first he had to get past Navin's receptionist. "She didn't know who I was. I told her, 'I'm Hank Greenberg. I'm on the team.'" Although he was nervous when he began to speak with Navin, Hank asked if the owner could let him go to another team—one where he could play every day. "Mr. Navin," Greenberg said, "I'll get fat just sitting on the bench."

"Have patience, young man," Navin told him. "You'll be playing before you know it, don't worry."

"So I sat there on the bench for about two more weeks, very unhappy," Greenberg recalled. "I'll never forget what happened next: one day we were just about ready to go out and start the ball game, when the phone rang in the manager's cubbyhole in the locker room. Bucky Harris answered it. Then he came out and went over to this big slate board, with the lineup on it, and erased Harry Davis' name and put mine in its place."

It did not take long for the young baseball player to attract attention. From the very beginning, the "big, awkward, gawky kid," as Greenberg described himself, could hit the ball out of the park. During his first season with the Tigers, Greenberg proved he deserved his place in the batting order. He played in 120 games and ended the season hitting over .300. Second baseman Charlie Gehringer was the only other Tiger to hit over .300 that season. Nicknamed the "Mechanical Man" because he was a consistent hitter, Gehringer was in his tenth season with the Tigers when Greenberg joined the team.

Together, Greenberg and Gehringer were about to energize the Tigers.

Greenberg was only nineteen years old in 1930, his first year with the Detroit Tigers. He was a "Jewish Babe Ruth" in a time and place where people were not accustomed to the idea of a Jewish baseball star.

5

THE JEWISH TIGER

HANK GREENBERG WAS NOT THE FIRST Jewish man to play in Major League Baseball, but he quickly became the most widely known. As Greenberg became a baseball star, Jews found the hero many of them had been hoping for since they had immigrated to America in large numbers during the early 1900s.

As soon as word got out that the Tigers' handsome new first baseman was Jewish—and single—Greenberg was invited to every Jewish event in the city. "My first year in Detroit, I had hardly made the team when the Jewish fans there wanted to give me a dinner and a Cadillac," Greenberg said. "I immediately turned it down. I knew that if I accepted an automobile, I would be obligated to every one of those fans who chipped in $10 or $20, and I didn't want to feel that they owned me." A well-known Jewish lawyer said that, as a young boy, he thought Hank would "become the first Jewish president." At Joe Muer's Fish House, one of Detroit's most popular restaurants, a corner table was reserved for Greenberg, and he was always taken care of by an extra waiter so that his meals would not be interrupted by Tiger fans. "Many times I'd go into Joe Muir's [sic] place and all the patrons would get up and give me a standing ovation. It was embarrassing and very heady stuff for a kid … I hope I didn't let it go to my head."

At the end of the 1933 season, there was no doubt about who played first base for the Detroit Tigers. After hitting over .300, including twelve home runs, the twenty-two-year-old had earned his position. When he returned home to New York at the end of the season, his family was eager to honor Hank's success. "There was a big family celebration when I got home, and then a big neighborhood celebration. All my pals were elated; my mother and father were overnight big shots," Greenberg said.

"Look at you," Sarah Greenberg said to her son. "The Napoleon of the Bronx!"

"I don't think anybody can imagine the terrific importance of Hank Greenberg to the Jewish

community," said one Detroit fan. "He was a God, a true folk hero." Some Jewish publications began referring to Greenberg as "the Jewish Babe Ruth."

However, there was also a growing feeling of anti-Semitism—in the United States and abroad—and Jewish Americans were still considered outsiders, especially when it came to America's favorite sport, baseball. The era was dominated by Babe Ruth. Ruth finished his twenty-one-year career with the Boston Braves in 1935, Greenberg's third season with the Tigers. "The Sultan of Swat," as Babe was called, led the New York Yankees to win seven American League pennants and four World Series titles. He also hit 714 home runs—with 60 home runs in one season.

Most of the fans at a Tigers game identified Greenberg as "the Jewish player." Sometimes, players from opposing teams used Greenberg's religion as an excuse to taunt the first baseman. "They always had a couple of guys in the dugout who were on me all the time," Greenberg recalled. "It got pretty nasty. One time they

Four of the game's greatest hitters in 1934, which was Babe Ruth's last season with the New York Yankees. From left to right: Hank Greenberg, Babe Ruth, Charlie Gehringer, and Lou Gehrig.

even brought up a player from the minor leagues just to give me a hard time. I thought I handled it pretty well. I never let them know they were getting to me. That way they would have won. But it wasn't easy."

Greenberg was quick to point out, though, that jeers and calls based on a player's background were common during the 1930s. "I could take it because I saw others getting it, too. Italians were 'wops,' Germans were 'Krauts,' and Polish players were 'dumb Polacks.' Me, I was a 'kike,' a 'sheenie,' or a 'mockie.' I was a good target. What made it tough is that there were a lot of Italians, Germans and Poles around, but I was the only Jew. They seemed to reserve a little extra for me."

Although Greenberg did not usually respond to the name calling, the frustration at times got the best of him. During one game, after being called a "Jew so and so" by a young Detroit teammate, Greenberg picked up a bat, "sidled up to the player in question with a wicked glint in his eye and warned him that 'if you so much as peep once again to me I'll bring this bat across your thick skull.'"

At the end of Greenberg's first season, the manager, Bucky Harris, was released by the Tigers and replaced by Mickey Cochrane. The Tigers were in fifth place in the American League, leaving only three teams with a worse record. Cochrane, the catcher for the Philadelphia Athletics since 1925, was to continue playing. During baseball's early years, it was common to have player-managers. Players who served this double duty both played their position and managed the game. Ty Cobb, the star hitter and center fielder, had spent the last six years of his twenty-one seasons with the Tigers as the club's player-manager.

Cochrane's dynamic and intense personality inspired the Tigers. He was an excellent catcher, and the players were confident that Cochrane, along with another new player, Leon "Goose" Goslin, could make the 1934 team more successful. "Listen," Cochrane told his new team, "we're going to win. We're not going to lose." Greenberg thought Cochrane and Goslin were just the kinds of players the Tigers needed, and he was hopeful about the 1934 season.

Greenberg responded to the Tigers' improved lineup. In 1934, he hit 26 home runs and 63 doubles, drove in 139 runs, and ended the season with a .339 average. "Hank, of course, was our big gun," said Gehringer. "He had long arms and a big arc to his swing, so even if he was fooled on a pitch he could still hit the ball a long ways. His [Greenberg's] famous saying to me was, 'Just get the runner over to third.' Hank loved those RBIs."

Now in his second season with the Tigers, Greenberg was maturing as a baseball player. His performance at the plate proved he had what it took to be Detroit's biggest star since Ty Cobb.

"Just about every morning I'd shag fly balls for Gehringer, Goslin, Greenberg, whoever ... Especially Greenberg," recalled one boy who spent summers living across the street from Navin Field. "... That Jew, boy ... I want to tell you something—he was not a good ball player. He made himself a good ball player from practice. He'd be out there in the morning for an hour and a half, two hours."

The 1934 American League pennant race came down to two teams: the New York Yankees and the Tigers. By mid-July, when the two teams met for a four-game series in Detroit, the Yankees were three and a half games ahead of the Tigers. At the end of the series, it was a different race. After winning three of the four games, the Tigers trailed by only one and a half games, and Greenberg provided the spark that changed his team's fortunes. "Henry Greenberg dealt the Yankees a crushing blow at Navin Field before 26,000 highly excited fans," reported the *New York Times*. H. G. Salsinger, the sports editor of the *Detroit News*, wrote: "The development of Greenberg is one of the most amazing features of an amazing baseball season. He was a good hitter last year and a long one, but today he is one of the most powerful sluggers who has come along in years."

Greenberg missed only one game during the 1934 season. That game, as he described it, "became a national issue." With the Tigers battling the Yankees for first place in the American League, every game mattered. But two important Jewish holidays took place at the end of the season in September.

The Tigers were scheduled to play the Boston Red Sox on September 10, which was also Rosh Hashanah, the Jewish New Year. Eight days later, on September 18, Yom Kippur, the Day of Atonement, they would face the Yankees.

Although Greenberg was not an observant Jew, he was in an awkward position. He wanted to honor his Jewish faith and his parents, but he also wanted to help his team at a critical time. Asked to comment on his son's dilemma, David Greenberg told a reporter for the *New York Evening Post*: "We are an Orthodox family. He promised us when we saw him in Philadelphia on Detroit's last trip to the East that he would not play on Rosh Hashanah or Yom Kippur."

Greenberg's teammates wanted him in the lineup. One Tigers pitcher said later, "I didn't know what Rosh Hashanah was. The papers said Hank wasn't going to play because it was a Jewish holiday … I was a little upset because I thought I'm going to pitch a ball game without Hank. I came from Kansas and I never knew what a Jew was. Never gave it a thought. I would say Hank was the first Jewish person I ever met."

After much debate—and conversations with Greenberg's parents and a Detroit rabbi—a compromise was reached. Greenberg would play on Rosh Hashanah, a day of celebration, but not on Yom Kippur, the holiest day of the year. "He [the rabbi] consulted the Talmud," said Hank Greenberg, "and announced that I could play on Rosh Hashanah, the Jewish New Year, because that was a happy occasion on which Jews used to play ball in the streets." The rabbi's decision put Hank back in the lineup. "I hit two home runs off Boston's Dusty Rhodes," Hank recalled. "We beat the Red Sox 2–1, with my second homer winning the game in the tenth inning. Just like in the movies, right?"

On Yom Kippur, just ten days after Rosh Hashanah, Greenberg spent the day in a synagogue rather than on a baseball diamond. When he walked into the crowded temple "everything seemed to stop," recalled Greenberg. "The rabbi looked up; he didn't know what was going on. And suddenly everybody was applauding. I was embarrassed: I didn't know what to do.

It was a tremendous ovation for a kid who was only 23 years old, and in a synagogue no less!" Making the day even better was the fact that his team won without him. The Tigers beat the Yankees 2–0.

H. G. Salsinger of the *Detroit News* praised Greenberg's decision. He is "the greatest player the Jews have contributed to baseball ... and an illustrious torch bearer of his people." Another reporter wrote that Greenberg is "in position to do untold good in breaking down the mean and vicious prejudices against an ancient and honorable people."

Poet Edgar Guest, whose work was published in newspapers across the country, even wrote a poem about Greenberg's holiday dilemma.

•   •   •

The Irish didn't like it when they heard of Greenberg's fame
For they thought a good first baseman should possess an Irish name;
And the Murphys and Mulrooneys said they never dreamed they'd see
A Jewish boy from Bronxville out where Casey used to be.
In the early days of April not a Dugan tipped his hat
Or prayed to see a "double" when Hank Greenberg came to bat.

In July the Irish wondered where he'd ever learned to play.
"He makes me think of Casey!" Old Man Murphy dared to say;
And with fifty-seven doubles and a score of homers made
The respect they had for Greenberg was being openly displayed.
But on the Jewish New Year when Hank Greenberg came to bat
And made two home runs off Pitcher Rhodes—they cheered like mad for that.

Came Yom Kippur—holy fast day world-wide over to the Jew—
And Hank Greenberg to his teaching and the old tradition true
Spent the day among his people and he didn't come to play.
Said Murphy to Mulrooney, "We shall lose the game today!
We shall miss him on the infield and shall miss him at the bat,
But he's true to his religion—and I honor him for that!"

•   •   •

"I was a hero around town, particularly among the Jewish people," Hank said later, "and I was very proud of it."

Greenberg (right) meets teammate Goose Goslin at the plate during the 1935 World Series. Note the "mascot" in the center of the picture. Prior to modern-day "fuzzy" baseball mascots, young boys served that function.

6

HAMMERIN' HANK

MICKEY COCHRANE DELIVERED ON HIS promise to make the Tigers a winning team and give the fans, many of them still suffering the hardships of the Great Depression, something to cheer about. The 1934 Tigers, led by the "G-Men," Greenberg, Gehringer, and Goslin, won 101 games and the American League pennant for the first time in twenty-five years. Next stop: facing the St. Louis Cardinals in the World Series.

During the early part of the twentieth century, St. Louis had grown into a major midwestern city, and its baseball team, the Cardinals, had one of the best rosters in the history of baseball. The Gashouse Gang, as they were called, was led by two dynamic pitchers, who were also brothers, Jay Hanna "Dizzy" Dean and Paul Dee "Daffy" Dean, along with several other

The Dean brothers were stars of the St. Louis Cardinals during the mid-1930s. This promotional shot of Jay Hanna "Dizzy" Dean (left) and Paul Dee "Daffy" Dean was taken in 1934.

players with memorable nicknames: Joe "Ducky" Medwick, James "Rip" Collins, John Leonard "Pepper" Martin, and Leo "the Lip" Durocher. Dizzy Dean was the star, though.

On the morning of October 2, a crowd gathered at the train station in Detroit to welcome Dean. Dizzy greeted them, waving his hat, before going to the hotel to mingle with celebrities in town for the next day's Series opener.

Game 1, played at Detroit's Navin Field, did not go so well for the home team. Perhaps overwhelmed by the excitement surrounding the Series, the Tigers' normally solid infield committed five errors. Greenberg himself admitted to feeling "so nervous I couldn't eat." St. Louis took advantage of their opponent's shaky start and won the first game 8–3 in front of a gloomy Detroit crowd.

The Tigers bounced back, winning an error-free Game 2 and tying the Series. The next three games were in St. Louis, but the Tigers won two of them and returned to Detroit with a 3–2 lead in the Series. With Daffy Dean on the mound, the Cardinals won Game 6, and the Series came down to one game.

"We had to start a rookie pitcher in the final game—Elden Auker," Greenberg recalled. "Dizzy shut us out," Greenberg said, after the Cardinals embarrassed the Tigers and won the Series by winning the final game 11–0.

After the Series was over, Tiger manager Mickey Cochrane paid a visit to the St. Louis clubhouse to congratulate Frankie Frisch, the manager of the Cardinals. "I'm happy for the National League that you don't have more than two Deans pitching," Cochrane said.

Greenberg was criticized for his poor World Series performance. "The Cardinals gave me hell," he said about his nine strikeouts. The Cardinals also gave Greenberg "hell" from their dugout. Frisch admitted that some of the players on the Cardinals' bench were rough on Greenberg.

Greenberg knew his regular-season numbers were one of the main reasons the Tigers made it to the Series in 1934—a fact the *New Yorker* magazine pointed out in an article calling him "the ablest Jew in baseball."

Greenberg also knew that the Tigers' owner, Frank Navin, would be in New York before the beginning of the 1935 season and decided to request a meeting with his boss to ask for a raise.

"I'd like to have $15,000," Greenberg told Navin when they met at the Commodore Hotel in Manhattan.

"Very well," the Tigers' owner said. "I'll give you a $10,000 contract and $5,000 bonus."

"I don't care how you do it," said Greenberg, "but my contract will be for $15,000 and that's where we'll start talking next season."

Navin agreed to a contract for ten thousand dollars, then took out his ledger, wrote a check for five thousand dollars, and handed it to the twenty-four-year-old player. "No way was I going to take any chance with that money," he said. "I lived way up in the Bronx and I had to take the subway home. I went into the bank and opened a savings account and deposited the whole $5,000."

Greenberg knew how lucky he was. "In 1935, that $15,000 was an awful lot of money … The economy hadn't blossomed that much, many people were still out of work, and very few salaries in the American League were higher than that. And here I had only finished my second year in the Major Leagues." Although few players earned as much as Greenberg, major league baseball players were still making far more money than most Americans.

Greenberg was a respected player and was treated like a hero in New York and Detroit. Besides negotiating a new contract during the off-season, Greenberg also agreed to play in an exhibition basketball game with the Brooklyn Jewels, a semipro team. When word got back to the Tigers' owner, Greenberg's basketball-playing days came to an end. "I notice in the papers that you are going to engage in basket-ball," Navin wrote to his star first baseman. "I wish you would look at your contract … The worst possible thing a person of your build … could do is to play basket-ball—in addition to the fact that it slows you up … Notwithstanding this," the letter continued, "you agreed not to play the game."

When he returned to Detroit for the 1935 season, Greenberg quickly earned the nickname "Hammerin' Hank" by hitting 36 home runs and batting in 170 runs. He proved he was worth his paycheck when he was unanimously voted the American League's Most Valuable Player. On top of that, Greenberg led his team to their second straight pennant. The Tigers were going back to the World Series.

Greenberg was not particularly superstitious, but there was someone he considered his "good luck charm" during the 1935 season. Joe Roginski was a bat boy for the Detroit Tigers, and like Greenberg, he sometimes felt like an outsider. Roginski was Polish and thought an "Irish-sounding" name would help him fit in better, so he used the last name of Roggin when he worked in the clubhouse. Greenberg warmed up before games by playing catch with Roggin and once, after hitting a home run in a game, the thirteen-year-old ran out to greet him at home plate. Roggin's brother later recalled that "Hank would come over and have a bowl of *czarnina*, duck blood soup. Word would get out and a half-hour later there was five hundred kids gathered outside."

Greenberg may have considered Roggin to be a lucky charm, but his luck ran out during the 1935 World Series against the Chicago Cubs. On October 2, Navin Field was crowded to capacity for the opening game, but the thirty-six thousand fans did not go home happy. Greenberg not only went hitless during the first game, but he was badly heckled from the Chicago bench. "… they started riding me, calling me Jew this and Jew that. Behind the plate was Umpire George Moriarty; he walked over to the Cubs' bench and told them to stop riding me. They said it was none of his [expletive] business and that they would ride me if they pleased."

Tuck Stainback, one of the players for the Cubs, remembered one of his teammates, Billy Jurges, shouting "Throw him a pork chop, he'll never hit it!" (For religious reasons, Jews do not eat pork.)

After a 3–0 loss in the first game, the Tigers began to turn things around the next day. On a cold and windy October day, with fans wrapped in blankets, the Tigers' bats came alive. In the first inning, with Gehringer

Greenberg couldn't avoid a home plate collision with Cubs catcher Gabby Hartnett during a game on October 3, 1935.

on base, Greenberg hit a two-run homer. And then, during the seventh inning, Greenberg got on first base after being hit by a pitch. When the next batter, Pete Fox, singled to right field, Greenberg was headed for third base, but when the ball was thrown to second in an attempt to tag out Fox, Greenberg decided to try to score.

"I slid into home plate," Greenberg recalled. "Gabby Hartnett had the plate blocked, and as he fell on me, my left wrist curled up against my body, and when I fell I snapped it back." Hartnett, the Cubs catcher, weighed two hundred pounds, and there were people in the bleachers who later said they could "hear the sound of the impact." Greenberg finished the game, helping his team claim an 8–3 victory, but soon felt horrible pain. X-rays showed that Greenberg sprained his wrist, and he spent the rest of the Series on the bench. It was, as he described it, "a keen blow to my aspirations to help the Tigers win the world championship after our loss in the Series the year before."

Even without Hammerin' Hank, the Tigers won their first World Series in the team's forty-one-year history. Goose Goslin, whose hit in the sixth game brought Mickey Cochrane home to win the Series, was carried into the dugout by cheering fans. Cochrane, the manager who reenergized a team and a city, came back onto the field to announce: "This is the greatest day of my life."

For Greenberg, further X-rays showed that he had actually broken two bones. He may have ended the season on the bench, but after it was announced that he was the American League's Most Valuable Player of 1935, Greenberg was now truly a star.

The 1935 World Series champions. After losing in 1907, 1908, 1909, and 1934, the Tigers finally won their first World Series. Greenberg is the last player on right, bottom row. Seated next to him is Joe Roginski, a bat boy for the Tigers, who Greenberg considered a "good luck charm."

The "Brown Bomber," Joe Louis. Louis was the world heavyweight boxing champion between 1937 and 1949.

7

SPORTS TAKE CENTER STAGE

IN 1935, THE EDITORS OF THE *DETROIT FREE PRESS*, the city's most widely read newspaper, doubled the size of the daily sports section. Three of Detroit's sports teams had certainly given them good reason to do so. Not only did the Tigers win their first World Series that year, but the Detroit Lions were the champions of the National Football League and the Detroit Red Wings won the National Hockey League's Stanley Cup.

There was also another sport making headlines in 1935—boxing. African American Joe Louis, a Detroit resident and known as the "Brown Bomber," was establishing himself as a heavyweight boxer. After ten years of winning minor fights, Louis turned professional in 1934 and won twelve

President Franklin D. Roosevelt was the thirty-second president of the United States. He was elected in 1932 and served until he died in office in 1945, right before the end of World War II. During the Great Depression of the mid-1930s, he encouraged Major League Baseball to continue playing as a boost to people's spirits.

contests in as many months. In 1935, he faced his toughest opponent to date, the Italian heavyweight Primo Carnera. The place was Yankee Stadium in New York City in front of sixty-two thousand people. Like Greenberg, Louis was an outsider. He also knew how much his fans counted on him. He represented something more important than boxing to his black fans, who were discriminated against and often treated as second-class citizens.

"They put a heavy weight on my twenty-year-old-shoulders," said Louis. "Now, not only did I have to beat the man, but I had to beat him for a cause." Louis won the fight and became the "toast of Harlem" and the best heavyweight in America.

While sports were commanding headlines, political events in Germany were becoming more frightening. Adolf Hitler consolidated his power by making his National Socialist German Workers' (Nazi) Party the only legal political organization in the nation, and established himself as *der Führer*, the supreme leader. For German Jews, life was getting harder every day. In 1935, Hitler instituted the Nuremberg Race Laws, which essentially made Jews noncitizens in the eyes of his Nazi regime. Hitler's plans didn't end at the German border. He wanted to expand his policies of fear and hate across all of Europe.

Back in Detroit, many people were not aware of the events taking place in Germany. They were focused on finding stable jobs and providing for their families. Like Germans who elected Hitler because he promised to put people back to work and make Germany strong again, Americans were also desperate for solutions to their hardships.

Many citizens had confidence in their president, Franklin D. Roosevelt. Since his election in 1932, Roosevelt had tackled the challenges of the Great Depression by establishing government-funded projects to employ workers. During his Fireside Chats, a series of evening radio broadcasts, he spoke reassuringly to Americans and encouraged them to remain hopeful.

While Roosevelt was using radio to calm people's fears, a Detroit-based Roman Catholic priest, Father Charles Coughlin, was using the airwaves for a different purpose. Coughlin began attaching a microphone to his pulpit in 1926, and by the early 1930s, his sermons were being broadcast nationwide by the Columbia Broadcasting System. The "Radio Priest," as Coughlin was called, used his platform to present his views on religion and politics. No one was immune from his mean-spirited sermons; Coughlin criticized Roosevelt, blamed Jewish business leaders for the economic crisis, and appealed to people's worst instincts. On the topic of growing tensions in Germany, Coughlin described Jews as "a powerful minority in their influence, a minority endowed with an aggressiveness and initiative which, despite all obstacles, has carried their sons to the pinnacles of success in journalism,

Father Charles Coughlin, the "Radio Priest," reached an audience of more than forty million listeners with his weekly radio broadcasts.

in radio, in finance, in all science and arts."

In the same town where Coughlin was preaching messages of intolerance and anti-Semitism, one of the most prominent athletes in the country—a Jewish baseball player—was looking forward to the 1936 season. The first order of business for Greenberg and his teammates was to adjust to new ownership. Frank Navin had died only five weeks after his team won their first World Series, and Walter O. Briggs, a millionaire industrialist, was the new man in charge. Briggs had lost the use of his legs after contracting polio as a young man. Although his mobility was limited, Briggs was a tough negotiator, and one of his first challenges was renewing his first baseman's contract.

Greenberg was offered twenty-five thousand dollars per year, but he wanted thirty-five thousand. "For the first and only time in my baseball career, I became an official holdout," said Greenberg. "When spring training started, I was among the missing." Greenberg's demand for a higher salary was the sports talk of Detroit. A local newspaper article reported: "Greenberg's fight for more dough was the first serious affair of this nature to stir up Tiger fans since the days of Ty Cobb."

It wasn't too long before Greenberg was invited down to Florida to visit the new owner's winter home. Mickey Cochrane, who took part in the discussions, was annoyed, according to Greenberg. "My response was that if he [Cochrane] wasn't getting $35,000, then he wasn't getting paid enough."

Ultimately, Greenberg, eager to get back to the ball field, accepted the twenty-five thousand dollars he was offered. "All I was trying to do was establish my point," he recalled. "If I could play ball and have good seasons, I knew that eventually I'd make up that extra $5,000 that I may have gotten in a compromise."

Greenberg got off to a terrific start. But just twelve games into the season, he collided with a player from the Washington Senators and cracked one of the same bones in his left wrist that he had hurt in the 1935 World Series. Greenberg was out for the rest of the season. During his absence, the New York Yankees, playing in their first World Series since Babe Ruth's retirement, went on to win the 1936 Series against the New York Giants.

In the summer of 1936, another major sporting event was taking place in Berlin—the Olympic Games. But when the Nazi Party excluded German Jewish athletes from participating in the Games, many angry American athletes threatened to boycott the Olympics. The Olympics, the Americans argued, should promote good sportsmanship and fairness, and barring Jewish athletes would be inconsistent with those values.

But the Amateur Athletic Union of the United States voted for U.S. participation in the Games, and more than three hundred Americans, nineteen of whom were African American, participated. Among the black athletes was track star Jesse Owens, who went on to win four gold medals and became one of the Games' heroes.

Jewish athletes, including seven Jewish American men, did compete in the Games. But even the Germans, in response to pressure from the

International Olympic Committee, invited a Jewish woman, a fencer named Helene Mayer, to participate. Mayer won a silver medal.

On the day before the men's 4x100 relay race, two Jewish members of the American team were replaced. Twenty-one-year-old Sam Stoller later described the incident as the "most humiliating episode" in his life. Their coaches said the decision to bench him and his teammate, Marty Glickman, was based purely on selecting the fastest runners for the race. However, both Stoller and Glickman had beaten one of the other American runners previously. Many observers believed that the person responsible for the last-minute change was not the track coach but Avery Brundage, president of the United States Olympic Committee and a strong supporter of American

Hitler (center left) and Nazi officials salute during the opening ceremony of the 1936 Olympic Games in Berlin.

participation in the Berlin Olympics. Brundage, many believed, did not want to put his German hosts in the awkward position of awarding medals to two Jewish athletes.

Germany won more medals than any other country at the Berlin games, but the Summer Olympics were tainted by the policies of hatred and intolerance of the Nazi Party.

It wouldn't be long before the horrors of Kristallnacht, a well-planned violent campaign to intimidate Jews and destroy their culture, would show the entire world the true intentions of Hitler and his Nazi followers.

Track athlete Jesse Owens won four gold medals in the 1936 Summer Olympics. His medals were seen not only as athletic victories but also as a response to Hitler, who viewed the Olympics as an opportunity to showcase the talents of Aryan athletes.

A Detroit Tigers' publicity shot of Hank Greenberg taken around 1936–1937.

8

GREENBERG CHALLENGES THE RECORD

ONCE AGAIN, GREENBERG BEGAN A NEW baseball season with salary negotiations. But this time was different. The 1935 MVP was signed to a one-dollar-a-year contract. After spending the previous season on the bench with a broken wrist, he had to go through spring training to prove he was worth his regular twenty-five-thousand-dollar salary. "I was full of confidence and feeling that I would have no difficulty regaining my batting eye, and I went down to spring training with the contract and proved that I could play." By the beginning of the season, Greenberg was back at first base.

Greenberg would say that 1937 was his best as a baseball player—with 40 home runs, a batting average of .337, and 183 runs batted in (one short of the American League record set by Lou Gehrig in 1931). He was also selected to participate in a new baseball tradition—the All-Star Game. The 1937 game was the fifth time that the best players in the American and National leagues had faced one another. Nearly thirty-two thousand fans at Griffith Stadium, the home of the Washington Senators, were on hand to see President Franklin Roosevelt throw the ceremonial first pitch and Lou Gehrig hit the game's only home run.

During the season, Greenberg batted behind his friend and teammate Charlie Gehringer. "If we had a man on first base and Charlie was up, I'd yell, 'Get him to third, Charlie, just get him to third. I'll get him in,'" Greenberg recalled. And he did.

Greenberg also had a new teammate in 1937, Rudy York. York and Greenberg quickly proved to be a dangerous combination. "With him

The 1937 American League All-Stars, from left to right: Lou Gehrig (New York Yankees), Joe Cronin (Boston Red Sox), Bill Dickey (New York Yankees), Joe DiMaggio (New York Yankees), Charlie Gehringer (Detroit Tigers), Jimmie Foxx (Boston Red Sox), and Hank Greenberg. Major League Baseball's first All-Star Game was played in 1933. Until the 1947 game, the managers of the American League team and the National League team selected the players.

[York] behind me," said Greenberg, "I get more good balls to hit, pitchers are not so ready to walk me, knowing that the next batter they have to face is likely to hit the ball out of the park."

For Mickey Cochrane, however, 1937 was not a good year. The season before, overwhelmed by the demands of serving as the team's manager and catcher, Cochrane suffered a nervous breakdown. Then on May 25, 1937, things got worse. During the fifth inning of a game at Yankee Stadium, Cochrane was at bat with his head covered only by his cloth baseball cap. Cochrane "lost sight of the ball," and it "crashed into his left temple with a moist, sickening sound." Cochrane was carried off the field by four of his teammates and rushed to the hospital. X-rays showed that Cochrane had a triple fracture of the skull, a cracked right sinus, and a mild cerebral concussion. Two weeks in a New York hospital were followed by six weeks at Henry Ford Hospital in Detroit. Cochrane returned to the Tigers in time to see his team finish in second place—to the New York Yankees.

As he did every year, Greenberg returned to New York at the end of the season, where, according to the *Detroit Jewish Chronicle*, he brought "fame and credit to the Jewish people." Many of his young Jewish fans in Detroit wished he would stay there during the off-season. One fan wrote to the *Chronicle* suggesting that Greenberg be made the athletic director of a Jewish center in the city so that "all the Jewish boys of Detroit would nag their parents until they were allowed to join." The letter went on to say that boys "can do nothing better than to worship a young man like Hank Greenberg, a clean-minded, clean-living and an ideal man for the leadership of boys."

After the 1937 season, Greenberg now had fans all over the country, including players from opposing teams. Tommy Henrich, a longtime outfielder for the New York Yankees, played in many games against the Tigers. "On real good ball clubs," he said, "there's usually a guy that you can lean on a little bit, and that's what Hank Greenberg was to the Tigers. He was big, he was important, and they could lean on Greenberg."

Another fan of Greenberg's was the boxing champion Joe Louis. By 1937, Louis was far more than a boxer. Just as Greenberg carried the hopes and dreams of many first-generation Jewish immigrants, Louis and the Olympic track star Jesse Owens were idols to black Americans and symbols of their struggle for equality. In 1936, the same year Jesse Owens won four gold medals in Berlin, Louis faced—and was defeated by—the white German boxer Max Schmeling. Hitler and his supporters seized upon Schmeling's victory to make the boxer the "Nazi party's darling."

German boxer Max Schmeling (right) jabs American Joe Louis during their 1936 match at Yankee Stadium in New York. The fight between the two heavyweight champions took place against the backdrop of Hitler's rise to power in Germany and was enormously symbolic. Schmeling won the 1936 match but was defeated by Louis when the two men met again in 1938.

"I know you won it for Germany. We are proud of you. Heil Hitler," wrote one of Hitler's top aides to Schmeling. Soon after the fight, in fact, Hitler invited Schmeling to a lunch in his honor, during which the Führer asked Schmeling if he knew he would "beat the Negro."

Two years later, in June 1938, while Greenberg was well into his fifth season with the Tigers and Hitler was planning to invade other countries and strengthen Germany's position in Europe, a rematch took place between the two great heavyweights. President Roosevelt, who knew how much a Louis victory would mean to Americans, said to the boxer, "We need muscles like yours to beat Germany."

Both boxers were under intense pressure. NBC carried the fight live on 146 of its radio stations. A popular chain of stores, counting on increased sales, advertised its new Zenith Superheterodyne radio for $14.95. In Germany, Schmeling's wife was invited to the home of a high-ranking Nazi official to listen to the fight on radio there. For other Germans, the Nazi-imposed curfew was lifted for the evening so that cafés and bars could remain open.

In a packed Yankee Stadium, in front of seventy thousand fans, Louis denied the Nazi Party any opportunity to use Schmeling as a poster boy for Hitler's prejudices. Louis beat the German in a one-round fight—lasting two minutes and four seconds. In Detroit, Louis's hometown, a celebration in the streets included the unveiling of a banner that read "Joe Louis Knocked Out Hitler."

On the same night that Detroit fans were celebrating their hometown boxer's victory, the Tigers beat the Boston Red Sox in a newly improved Navin Field. Walter Briggs spent over one million dollars during the Great Depression to renovate the Tigers' home. Nearly twenty thousand seats were added to the ball park, renamed Briggs Stadium for the team's new owner, in order to hold fifty-three thousand fans. Only Yankee Stadium had more seats.

As it turned out, it was a good time to include more seats. The season itself was not remarkable. In fact the Tigers would finish in fourth place in 1938. But "Hammerin' Hank" was hitting home runs, and by late in the season, he was on course to break one of baseball's most sacred records—Babe Ruth's sixty home runs in a single season. By September 11, Greenberg had hit forty-nine of them, and everywhere he went, people were taking notice—even the record holder himself. "The strain is too great," Ruth said. "The boys are forever reminded about that record and it is bound to tell on them. It's telling on Greenberg now."

"I knew he was under a lot of pressure and he was nervous about it," said Charlie Gehringer. "I rode with him on the train one time and we were

With forty-five home runs under his belt, Hank Greenberg takes aim at number forty-six on August 30, 1938, during a game at Yankee Stadium.

talking about it. You could see that it was in him. I assume it even kept him awake nights, but he never really said that."

Another teammate, talking to a newspaper reporter, said, "He walks up and down the dugout during batting practice telling everybody that he isn't worrying about it, isn't even thinking about it. But he's thinking about it all the time and probably pressing too hard out there …"

To make matters worse, Greenberg didn't have the on-field support from catcher Mickey Cochrane. Cochrane never fully recovered from his injuries, and before the home run race heated up in September, he was gone. After nearly five seasons with the team, the player-manager was released from the Tigers organization. A Detroit reporter wrote that Cochrane "was close to tears as he shook hands with Detroit players."

Del Baker, formerly the Tigers' third-base coach and now the team's new manager, stood watch as Greenberg kept hitting home runs. Greenberg was getting tired—from the long season and the constant questions about Ruth's record. "I've heard that question so much … that I even hear it now in my sleep … ," he said.

By September 26, Greenberg's home run total stood at fifty-eight with five games left to play. "Greenberg," reported the Associated Press, "is within striking distance" of Babe Ruth's all-time record.

The next two games were played against the St. Louis Browns in Detroit. Greenberg thought he had a pretty good shot at breaking the record, but the first game with the Browns did not increase his confidence. Facing Bobo Newsom, a pitcher going for his twentieth win of the season, Greenberg left the stadium empty-handed. "He always kept the ball away from me, and I didn't quite have the power to go to right field and hit a home run," Greenberg recalled.

Greenberg's chances did not improve the next day. He walked twice and hit a ball to the left-field roof that was foul by a couple of feet. Greenberg left the stadium with three games remaining and three home runs needed to break the record.

Attention on Greenberg was mounting. His mother promised him sixty-one baseball-shaped gefilte fish if he broke the record. Newspaper reporters were watching every time Greenberg stepped up to the plate, and baseball fans around the country were taking notice. Comparing the events in Detroit with the increasingly bad news from Germany, the *Detroit Times* reported: "There is no shuffle of marching feet, no roar of armored tanks down well-paved streets …[no] frightening banners of war and all its ghastly consequences. But in Detroit at least the question still is, 'Can he make it?'"

Jewish fans especially were excited about their hero's chance to break the most important and widely known sports record. "They could deny Jewish boys the right to swim in a pool, but they couldn't deny the fact that a Jewish boy was close to breaking Babe Ruth's record," said one fan.

By this time, the Nazis had taken over Czechoslovakia and were putting more severe limits on the everyday lives of Jewish people. Greenberg was well aware that events abroad increased the pressure on him to break Ruth's record. "Being Jewish did carry with it a certain responsibility," he said. "After all, I was representing a couple of million Jews among a hundred million gentiles … I didn't pay much attention to Hitler at first or any of the political going-ons at the time … Of course, as time went by, I came to feel that if I, as a Jew, hit a home run, I was hitting one against Hitler."

A *New York Post* reporter connected events in Europe with Greenberg's home run race. "In Europe," he wrote, "they are asking, 'What is Hitler going to do?' I cannot answer that any more than can those experts who are wasting so much space nowadays trying to reach a sane conclusion concerning an insane man … In America the question is, 'Can Greenberg do it?' There's some sense in that."

For the pitchers, facing Greenberg was complicated, too. Some of them did not want to be the one throwing the pitch breaking Ruth's record. Browns catcher Billy Sullivan, who was behind the plate during the series with the Tigers, remembered that pitchers responded differently. "He's not going to break a record with my name in the paper," one of them told

Sullivan. Another pitcher said to Greenberg: "You're not going to get any home runs off me you Jew son of a bitch." Of course, not every player felt that way. "Hank, it's not going to hurt me," another pitcher told him. "I'll ease up."

Against the Indians, with three games left in the season, movie cameras were set up inside Cleveland's Municipal Stadium. But Denny Galehouse, the pitcher in the first game, had other plans. Galehouse pitched, according to Greenberg, "the greatest game of his life," which the Tigers lost 5–0. After striking out four times, Greenberg was clearly frustrated. He was "so mad that he kicked bats off the rack in front of the Tiger dugout to relieve his feelings," the *Detroit Free Press* reported.

The next day, Sunday, was a doubleheader. Bob Feller, the pitcher for the first game, was one of the best. Nineteen years old, Feller was already in "a class by himself," said Greenberg. Feller knew what he was up against and said he would "make Greenberg earn any home runs he hit off me." It was overcast on Sunday, and Greenberg remembered that "seeing the ball was difficult." In fact, all of the Tigers seemed to have trouble seeing the ball that day. Feller struck out eighteen players, setting a major league record. "I did get a double off him … That was the best I could do off Feller," said Greenberg. The Tigers lost the first game 4–1.

Greenberg's chance to break Ruth's record came down to one game. The Indians and the fans knew Greenberg could do it. He had hit two home runs in each of eleven different games that season. "It kept getting darker and darker," Greenberg said. Most stadiums, including Cleveland's, did not have lighting for night games, and so it was difficult for the players and the umpires to see. The game was called after seven innings. George Moriarty, the umpire, said to Greenberg, "I'm sorry, Hank. But this is as far as I can go."

I said, "That's all right, George, this is as far as I can go, too."

Greenberg with Lou Gehrig, the star first baseman for the New York Yankees in the 1930s. Greenberg was discouraged from pursuing a position with his hometown team after watching Gehrig at first base in 1929.

9

PLAYING IN
THE OUTFIELD

AFTER THE SEASON WAS OVER, COLLIER'S magazine invited Greenberg to write about the 1938 home run race. "First of all, you're tired," he wrote. "You've already played 140 games and that daily pounding has taken its toll. Second, the weather is cooler and the ball is less lively than it is in very warm weather. Third, the sun goes down earlier and the shadows are longer. The ball coming from the pitcher has to pass through the shadow and it is harder to follow."

Despite the way things turned out, Greenberg was proud of his accomplishment. "I still had 58 home runs alongside my name," he wrote in *Collier's*. "I was satisfied. Any time I can come within hailing distance of any Babe Ruth record I feel good about it."

There were others, players and fans, who wondered if there was another reason Greenberg was unable to break Ruth's record. Billy Rogell, the Tigers' shortstop, thought that Greenberg was often walked intentionally in the final games of the season. "I don't think just because he was Jewish, but that had a lot to do with it," said Rogell. He also went on to say that Greenberg's Tiger teammates were "pulling for him." "He was one of us," said Rogell.

Greenberg dismissed the stories that his religion played a part in the home run race. Instead, he told the story of a St. Louis player, George McQuinn, who dropped a foul ball on purpose so that Greenberg had a chance to add another home run to his total.

After the season ended, Greenberg returned to New York. The fall of 1938 gave him the rare opportunity to spend time with his brother Joe, who was now a third baseman in the minor leagues. "We used to go down to Broadway and play handball and have dinner and go to a show or just browse around. It was a new experience for us, from living in the Bronx and then having all that free time, no more school, money in our pockets. We thought we had the world by the tail," said Greenberg.

Greenberg did have "money in his pocket." One reporter described him as "an enormously impressive figure, physically ... richly and tastefully clothed, and so good-looking that you can hear the girls give quick little gasps as he walks by." "I was young and up and coming," Greenberg said, "and I guess people expected I'd hit 58 home runs the next season as well." By the start of the 1939 season, he was making forty thousand dollars per year—the highest-paid player in the major leagues.

A high-profile star, twenty-eight-year-old Greenberg was considered an eligible bachelor, and he dated a number of women, especially in New York during the off-season. One newspaper society column wrote: "Hank has been connected up with dozens of local debs and chorus gals and society leaders ... but they're still wrong and he's still single." Greenberg may not have been in any hurry to settle down, but his parents were eager for their son to be "married to some nice, quiet girl from a nice, quiet family," as his father told a newspaper reporter.

Greenberg's busy baseball life left little time for an active social life.

"I rarely went out," he said later. "I had a lot of married friends living in Detroit at the time, and I'd go to their homes for dinner and every once in a while someone would try to fix me up with a young lady, but I was basically wrapped up in the game …"

As soon as spring training began for the 1939 season, there were rumors that Lou Gehrig, the Yankees' first baseman, was not doing well, that he seemed "sluggish." Greenberg and his teammates "took it all with a grain of salt." "We knew," Greenberg said, "that once the season started Lou would be his old natural self as the backbone of the Yankee ball team."

That was not to be. Gehrig played uncharacteristically poor baseball during the early part of the season. Then on May 2, 1939, after 2,130 consecutive games, he took himself out of the lineup before a game in Detroit

The 1939 Detroit Tigers. Greenberg is in the top row, fifth from the left.

After playing first base his entire career, Greenberg moved to the outfield in 1940.

with the Tigers. Gehrig did not play again. Greenberg saw Gehrig in mid-May when the Tigers had their next game with the Yankees. By this time, it was public knowledge that Lou Gehrig, the player known as "The Iron Horse," suffered from amyotrophic lateral sclerosis, a fatal disease. Gehrig was sitting on the bench, and Greenberg saw a dramatic difference. "His hair had turned white almost overnight and he could barely drag his leg up the stairs of the dugout … It was pitiful to see what had happened in two weeks' time."

Although the 1939 Tigers had a record of 81 wins and 73 losses, they finished the season in fifth place. "While I didn't have a sensational year, I still led the team in hitting, with a .312 average; had 112 runs batted in, which was fourth in the American League, and hit 33 home runs, which was second in the league only to Jimmie Foxx, who hit 35. So it wasn't a total disaster as far as my personal record was concerned," said Greenberg.

The 1940 season began with a major change in the infield. Greenberg's teammate Rudy York had proved his abilities as a slugger in 1937 when he hit thirty-five home runs and batted .307. His fielding performance was the

The 1940 Detroit Tigers line up in the dugout. Greenberg is the fourth player from the right, between Rudy York (on his right) and Charlie Gehringer (on his left).

problem. The Tigers had bounced York around several positions, all without success. Jack Zeller, the team's general manager, along with manager Del Baker, had one other position they wanted York to try—first base.

While he was in New York for the off-season, Greenberg was asked to return to Detroit to meet with Zeller. "The sum and substance of the conversation was that Jack wanted me to try the outfield," remembered Greenberg. Zeller explained that the team did not want to lose York in the lineup, but they had tried him at three or four other positions and they didn't work. For Greenberg, who had played first base for seven years, it was a "complete surprise."

After thinking about it for a few days, Greenberg persuaded Zeller to give him a ten-thousand-dollar bonus if he made the switch successfully. "I was strong. I was twenty-nine years old and in the prime of my life, and I loved to play," he said. "I really could stay out in that outfield all day and shag flies … After a while I started to improve; I learned to judge balls and then it became a matter of learning to play the hitters."

Barney McCosky, the Tigers' center fielder, heard from his teammate right away. "I need a little help in the outfield," Greenberg said to McCosky. The two players arranged to meet at the park for a few early morning practice sessions. "I would throw balls up against the fence and holler at him, 'Second base!' 'Third base!'…We did that for maybe four straight days," recalled McCosky.

One day, after one of McCosky's private outfield lessons, Greenberg asked his teammate to meet him downtown at a tailor's workshop. Greenberg asked the tailor to make a suit for McCosky. "I couldn't believe it," recalled McCosky. "I never had no hundred-dollar suit. I would pay about $38 to $45. And he bought me a tailor-made suit. I didn't know material, but I know it fit good."

Greenberg got tips from one of his competitors as well. Joe DiMaggio was the star center fielder for the New York Yankees, but he was more than happy to help his friend Greenberg. DiMaggio and Greenberg had known each other for many years. "I used to see Joe at Toots Shor's restaurant in New York. I'd meet him there and we'd have lunch and sit

Greenberg helps remove fruits and vegetables that were thrown on the field during the 1940 American League Championship game in Cleveland. The Tigers beat the Indians 2–0 and clinched the American League title.

around all afternoon talking about baseball, even though he wasn't a big conversationalist," Greenberg recalled later.

One of Greenberg's concerns was learning when to run in for a fly ball hit to the outfield. DiMaggio told him not to come in too fast. "You have to try to float in," he told him.

Greenberg was praised for agreeing to change positions. A *New York American* reporter wrote: "Hank did something that few ballplayers would do … He gave up a position in which he was an outstanding star, and which he preferred to play, for the good of the Detroit team … 999 ballplayers out of a thousand, I think, would have, in Greenberg's place, gone on playing first base, permitting York and the Detroit management to worry about York … Had he been any of the sort of guy except the sort of guy he is, the only way they would have gotten him off of it would have been to trade him."

During his first year as the Tigers' left fielder, Greenberg made fifteen fielding errors. His hitting, however, did not suffer from the move. He batted a career-high .340 and hit forty-one home runs.

Greenberg quickly grew to love the outfield. It was,

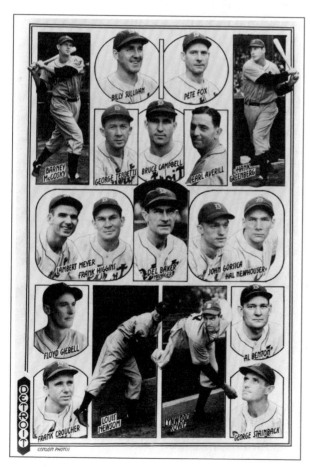

A promotional piece for the 1940 World Series champions. Hank Greenberg is in the upper right-hand corner, and manager Del Baker is in the center.

he said, "a lot easier than playing first base." But there was another reason he was happy with his new position. "I didn't have to take as much riding from the opposing players. In Detroit, first base is next to the *visiting* team's bench, so I was always fielding my position close to the opposition's yelling … I guess I had rabbit ears, because I often let what I heard bother me."

But Greenberg admitted to missing the excitement of first base and arguing with umpires over close calls. The outfield was quieter. "It's like a Broadway traffic cop being transferred out to Staten Island," Greenberg said.

To top off the season, Greenberg was voted Most Valuable Player of the American League for the second time—the first player to win the award at two different positions. "I can't say that I won it in 1940 for my fielding," said Greenberg. "I'm sure hitting had a great deal to do with it."

Greenberg's hitting also had a lot to do with the Tigers winning the 1940 American League pennant and returning to their first World Series since 1935. Their National League opponent was the Cincinnati Reds. Swept in the 1939 World Series by the New York Yankees, the Reds were motivated to win.

The Tigers went into the Series favored to win even though many of their best players were older. Although he was playing well, Gehringer was now thirty-seven years old. "Gehringer is probably being held together with adhesive tape, safety pins and fancy stitching," wrote a reporter for the *New York World-Telegram*. But one newspaper story, commenting on the matchup, said, "There's no antidote for Hank Greenberg's hitting."

Greenberg's hitting was not a factor in the Series. His only home run came in Game 5, and after Game 6, the Tigers and Reds were tied at 3–3. On October 8, the deciding game was played at Crosley Field in Cincinnati. Again, Greenberg wasn't able to make a difference. In four at bats, he had just two singles, and the Tigers lost the Series. "What a disappointed lot we were coming back from Cincinnati on that train, losing the final game after a long, hard season," said Greenberg. When the team pulled into the Michigan train depot, they were greeted by thousands of fans, which Greenberg said "made us feel a little better."

Greenberg joined the U.S. Army as a private. A year later, he was an officer, seen here in uniform, in the Army Air Force.

10

A NEW UNIFORM

BY THE BEGINNING OF 1941, HITLER'S campaign to control Europe seemed unstoppable, and his sights were now set on conquering Russia. The year before, his army invaded Norway, Denmark, Holland, and France. Throughout 1940, the United States had been able to stay neutral, but it was becoming increasingly clear that the country could not escape entering the war.

Sixteen million American men between the ages of twenty-one and thirty-five were required to register for the draft. Greenberg registered on his way back to New York after the 1940 World Series.

Returning from a Hawaiian vacation in mid-February, before the start of 1941 spring training, Greenberg was shocked to learn that his draft number was one of the first to be called. Immediately, sports reporters wanted to know if Greenberg would ask to start his military service on a later date. "What's all the fuss about? You'd think I was the only guy going into the army," he said. "I'm not going to ask for any kind of deferment. All I'm going to say is that when my number is up I'm going …"

On May 6, 1941, Hank Greenberg, now earning fifty-five thousand dollars per year, hit two home runs in a game against the Yankees. The following morning, he reported to an army unit at Fort Custer in Battle Creek, Michigan, where, as a private, he earned twenty-one dollars per month.

Greenberg (wearing a light suit and tie, second row, second from the left) arrives for training at Fort Custer in Michigan.

Greenberg's life changed overnight. "I was thirty years old, and I was in with a lot of roughnecks. These were guys who hadn't worked on the outside, who had been in the army for fifteen or twenty years."

One month after Private Greenberg reported for duty, U.S. senator Josiah Bailey of North Carolina used Greenberg's story as an example for others. "To my mind he's a bigger hero than when he was knocking home runs," Senator Bailey said. The popular magazine *Sport* later described Private Greenberg: "Through it all, Greenberg retained his good nature. He grinned at everybody, kidded with his fellow draftees, refused an invitation to become the leader of his induction group, and won the fierce loyalty of all the GIs on the post when he countered an officer's outstretched hand with a polite, formal salute. Hank was in the army now, but he was the same old Greenberg."

There wasn't much time for baseball at Fort Custer where Greenberg was now part of the Fifth Division, Second Infantry. Greenberg's fellow soldiers always invited him to join their pickup games, but most of the time, he opted to read or do army chores. However, Abe Bernstein, a friend from Detroit, coaxed him into playing one exhibition game between a group from Fort

Captain Hank Greenberg meets with two young fans.

Custer and a group of prisoners. When the army team arrived at the state prison, they realized that the uniform loaned to Greenberg did not fit him. But he did fit into a prison uniform. "Well, as long as I've got this uniform on, I might as well play with you guys," he said. Greenberg had not played baseball in over a month, but he hit a home run that sailed out over the prison yard. The prisoners all offered to help. "I'll get it! I'll get it!" they shouted.

Along with Greenberg's home run, he hit a double and two singles and led his team to win. "I got a big hand from the prisoners," Greenberg recalled.

While Greenberg was in the army, his absence was being felt at Briggs Stadium. Without their big hitter, the Tigers couldn't put runs on the scoreboard—or fans in the seats. During the 1941 season, attendance at Briggs Stadium dropped six hundred thousand—and the Tigers ended the season twenty-six games behind the Yankees.

Greenberg was in the army for only three months when the military's age requirement changed, and men over twenty-eight years old were no longer drafted. Greenberg had missed only one baseball season, and he hoped that he could rejoin the Tigers in the spring of 1942.

It took four months for Greenberg to be released from the army. He was discharged on December 5, 1941. "I headed back to Detroit, hoping that I could get myself ready for the 1942 season, but that Sunday morning, on December 7, all my plans were changed when the Japanese bombed Pearl Harbor," remembered Greenberg. "That changed the lives of everybody in the United States and around the world."

Japan's surprise attack on the U.S. Naval Base at Pearl Harbor left no doubt that America would now enter World War II. The following day, December 8, 1941, President Roosevelt announced that America was in a "state of war" with the Japanese Empire. While some sports writers wondered if Greenberg would return to the army, to Greenberg, it was not an option. "Baseball is out the window as far as I'm concerned," he said. "I don't know if I'll ever return to baseball."

A reporter for the *Sporting News* suggested that as the son of immigrants, Greenberg was inspired to reenlist. "But all the time there lay before Greenberg a picture," the article read. "His father and mother had come to this country from Rumania because the way of living there did not correspond to their ideas of going through life … Their son had an equal opportunity with the sons of all other people in this country."

This time around, Greenberg signed up for the Army Air Force. "I had my fill of the infantry," he said. He reported to MacDill Field in Tampa, Florida, where he remained until July 1942 when he was sent to the Officer Candidate School in Miami, Florida. After earning the rank of second lieutenant, he was assigned to the Flying Training Command in Fort Worth, Texas. For the next year and a half, he traveled around the United States inspecting training programs. But it wasn't long before he decided that, rather than spending his military career based in Fort Worth, he wanted to try an overseas post.

Greenberg's overseas assignment took him first to India, then to Burma and China. After another promotion, Greenberg was now a captain and served as the administrative commanding officer of the first group of B-29 bombers

Fans cheer at Briggs Stadium in 1942. After Pearl Harbor in December 1941, Greenberg reenlisted in the military, which caused him to miss the 1942 season.

based in Asia. "I'll never forget the first mission our B-29s made from our base to Japan," Greenberg told a *New York Times* reporter. After taking his place in the control tower, the planes went off "with clock-like precision."

Things did not always operate so smoothly. Greenberg remembered an incident when one of the pilots "saw he wasn't going to clear the runway, tried to throttle down, but the plane went over on its nose at the end of the field." Greenberg and another officer "raced over to the burning plane to see if we could help rescue anyone. As we were running, there was a blast when the gas tanks blew and we were only about 30 yards away when the bomb went off. It knocked us right into a drainage ditch alongside the rice paddies while pieces of metal floated down out of the air." Greenberg was unable to talk or hear for a few days following the explosion, but he was not hurt. "The miraculous part of it all was that the entire crew escaped," he said.

He was called back to the United States in the middle of 1944 and given a new assignment. America and its allies were making progress against Germany, and Greenberg was posted right in New York City. Greenberg's job was to travel to New England and talk with the factory workers who had made some of the equipment and supplies that were used by American soldiers.

During this time, major league baseball games were still being played, although with fewer players. Besides Hank Greenberg, other stars of the game had joined the armed forces. Greenberg's teammate Charlie Gehringer, Joe DiMaggio, the Yankees' star who helped Greenberg get started in the outfield, and Boston Red Sox slugger Ted Williams were among the hundreds of players from the American and National leagues who were serving their country.

Even without the sport's biggest names drawing fans to the park, baseball continued to be America's favorite game. "I honestly feel that it would be best for the country to keep baseball going," said President Roosevelt. "These players are a definite recreational asset to at least 20 million of their fellow citizens—and that in my judgement is thoroughly worthwhile."

Baseball did its part to support the war effort. Receipts from selected games were donated to war-related charities, fans were encouraged to return foul balls hit into the stands for delivery to overseas troops, and "The Star-Spangled Banner," previously sung only on special occasions, was now played at the beginning of each game.

The war provided many people with a common purpose: defeating Hitler and his allies. The war also provided Detroit with an opportunity to rebound after the Great Depression. Detroit was in the center of the wartime economy, producing supplies and equipment for American forces. The automobile assembly lines were now making parts for bombers, trucks,

Greenberg visits with his parents in New York after returning from his service in the U.S. Army. Three days later, on June 19, 1945, he would return to the Tigers' lineup.

and aircraft called Mustang, Wildcat, Hellcat, and Lightning. A *New York World-Telegram* reporter wrote: "At the moment Detroit is just about the most amazing city in America. Practically all the big factories are working night and day, most of them geared high for armament production. As a result of the endless shifts of workers, the city never sleeps. Movies, barber shops, and places of entertainment stay open all night."

Germany surrendered on May 7, 1945, one week after Adolf Hitler killed himself in Berlin. Japan would not surrender for three more months, but for Hank Greenberg and thousands of other soldiers, the war was over.

After four years in the army, thirty-four-year-old Greenberg may have thought his baseball days were behind him. But after spending a few weeks getting back in shape, he returned to Detroit. "Nobody has ever attempted to resume baseball operations after so long a lapse," the *Sporting News* reported. One

Greenberg shows bandaged hands after returning to baseball when his military service ended.

Detroit newspaper celebrated Greenberg's return with a large advertisement reading: "A Great Soldier, a Great Ball Player, Welcome Back, Hank Greenberg."

Greenberg was now an American sports star, not a Jewish one. By the mid-1940s, Greenberg's name was on a Louisville Slugger bat, and a Wheaties cereal box featuring Greenberg's picture read: "'A big bowl of Wheaties every morning,' Hank reveals, 'is the Greenberg way to start off a swell day.'"

On July 1, 1945, fifty-five thousand fans crowded into Briggs Stadium to see Hammerin' Hank's first major league game in four years, one month, and twenty-four days. In the eighth inning, Greenberg gave the fans what they came for—a home run. "Everybody was cheering like mad. After four years in the service, the greeting was nice, but it didn't matter all that much to me. I was just glad to be back alive."

Greenberg's return energized the Tigers. He played seventy-eight games in 1945 and hit thirteen home runs. But it was the final pennant-deciding game against the Washington Senators that made him a baseball hero again. During the ninth inning, with the bases loaded, Greenberg hit a grand slam home run—and the Tigers were in the World Series. "I wasn't sure whether I was awake or dreaming," Greenberg said after the game.

"When we returned to Detroit there were thousands of people in the train station giving me a big hand. But the best part of that home run was hearing later what the Washington players said: 'Goddamn that dirty Jew bastard, he beat us again.' They were calling me all kinds of names behind my back, and now they had to pack up and go home, while we were going to the World Series."

The experience of returning to a World Series against the Chicago Cubs, the same team they beat in 1935, seemed a bit unreal to Greenberg. "I had been in the service in India the year before, listening to the World Series over Armed Forces Radio, and now I was preparing to play in the Series."

Although the Tigers won, the 1945 World Series was generally

The 1945 World Series champions. Once again, the Tigers faced the Chicago Cubs in a World Series matchup. After losing to the Cubs in 1907 and 1908, the Tigers beat the Cubs in 1935 and 1945 to win the World Series.

considered to be poorly played. Greenberg hit well, particularly in the sixth game when his solo home run tied a game that the Tigers ultimately lost after twelve long innings.

But Greenberg was thinking about more than baseball. While stationed in New York at the end of the war, Greenberg met Caral Gimbel, the daughter of the president and part owner of Gimbel Brothers and Saks Fifth Avenue department stores. Greenberg did not want to pressure the socially prominent thirty-year-old Gimbel, who was divorced, to go out with him. She recalled the first time he called to invite her to dinner. "He said, 'You don't have to feel pinned down to this. If something comes up that you would rather do, then we can switch it.'" During the following months, they spent much of their free time together.

Caral was an active member of New York's social scene and enjoyed horseback riding. "I had no knowledge of baseball," she said. "When we went to dinner anyplace, people would come up and ask for autographs and that annoyed him. It amused me. He was so nice to people."

Like the Greenberg family, the Gimbels were Jewish. Greenberg's parents, though, were more devout, which caused some tension for the young couple. Because of the religious differences and the fact that they came from different economic backgrounds, they decided to have a small wedding.

Before Greenberg had to report to spring training for the 1946 season, he and Caral went to St. Augustine, Florida, where they hoped to be married quickly. The plan did not go as smoothly as the young couple had hoped. Florida law required a thirty-day waiting period after applying for a marriage license. They could, however, be married by a justice of the peace in Georgia, so they drove across the state line into Brunswick and were married.

"We searched out the best restaurant in Brunswick and went to dinner ... That's how the 1946 season got under way," Greenberg said.

Greenberg with his wife, Caral, an accomplished and enthusiastic horsewoman.

Greenberg crosses the plate on September 24, 1946, after hitting one of his 331
career home runs.

11

A MOVE TO THE FRONT OFFICE

THE NEWS ABOUT GREENBERG'S MARRIAGE did not take long to reach his fans. In Detroit, teenage girls wore black bobby socks to mourn the end of Greenberg's status as the city's most eligible bachelor.

But being married was just one of many changes that affected Greenberg during the 1946 season. "I had seen a lot of things happen in the world, and I didn't think that baseball was the only thing in my life … I went to spring training not quite the same man I had been in previous years," he said.

One of the biggest changes he faced was returning to first base. Rudy York was traded to Boston, and the Tigers needed Greenberg back in his old position. Greenberg had grown to like left field and thought he was not as "agile or quick or nimble" as he was when he played first base early in his career.

Greenberg (right) and Boston Red Sox players Ted Williams (left) and Eddie Pellagrini are photographed in Boston's Fenway Park with John F. Kennedy in 1946. The future U.S. president was elected that year to represent Massachusetts' Eleventh Congressional District in the U.S. House of Representatives.

By August, Greenberg was considering retiring from baseball. "The years had taken their toll," he said. "The old legs didn't function. Up at bat, the pitchers that I used to be able to handle without difficulty were becoming harder all the time … everyone knew I was a high-priced ballplayer, and they expected more than I was able to produce."

As it turned out, 1946 was not a completely unsuccessful season for Greenberg. Although he batted under .300 for the first time in his major league career, he hit nine home runs in September. But by the end of the season, after the Red Sox won the American League pennant, Greenberg knew his days at first base were over. "He did not look so good on ground balls last year, so a shift is in order," his new manager, Steve O'Neill, told the *Sporting News*.

On a Saturday afternoon in January 1947, Greenberg was listening to his car radio when he heard that he was being sent to the Pittsburgh Pirates.

He was angry and sad. A telegram confirmed the news: "This is to inform you that your contract has been assigned to the Pittsburgh Club of the National League." Later that month, Greenberg, a two-time MVP and five-time All-Star, ended his career with the Tigers.

One group was especially sorry to see him go—the American League bat boys. A newspaper article titled "Greenberg Big Favorite with Batboys, Attendants," reported that many young stadium employees would miss the big home run hitter. "He sure is a swell gentleman," one Yankee Stadium bat boy said. "He never demanded anything. He was always polite." Another boy said, "The kids in the National League will like him. We hope he breaks the home run record this year."

In Greenberg's mind, though, there would be no more attempts to break Ruth's home run record. He and Caral had just celebrated the birth of their first child, Glenn, and Hank did not want to go to Pittsburgh and play for a National League team. Even after Greenberg told the Pirates' general manager, Roy Hamey, that he had no intentions of playing for another team, John Galbreath, an owner, invited Greenberg to discuss plans over lunch. "I don't want to talk you into playing," Galbreath said. "I just want to have lunch with you."

Convincing Greenberg to join the Pirates was exactly what Galbreath intended to do. Over the course of their conversation, the two men talked about how Pittsburgh could accommodate Greenberg. In the end, Galbreath agreed to pay Greenberg one hundred thousand dollars for one season, making him the highest-paid player in either league. Galbreath also told Greenberg he could fly, rather than take the long train rides, between cities and agreed to change the dimensions of Forbes Field to give Greenberg a home field advantage (for hitting). There was one other thing Greenberg asked the Pirates' owner: "If I ever did play for anybody [else]," Greenberg said, "they'd have to give me my outright release at the end of the season. I never want to hear on the radio again that I've been traded or sold." Galbreath's mission had been accomplished. Greenberg agreed to play one more season at first base. Later, Greenberg admitted to being relieved that he would play again. "Baseball was still in my blood and this was a new challenge for me," he said. "I was looking forward to it with great anticipation."

Early in the season, the Brooklyn Dodgers came to play the Pirates. This was no regular game. Every game the Dodgers played during the 1947 season was noteworthy. Their first baseman, Jackie Robinson, was the first African American to play Major League Baseball, and his appearance on the field sparked enthusiasm and controversy. Prior to Robinson's joining the Dodgers, baseball's "color line" dictated that Major League Baseball teams were made up of whites only. Black players like Robinson played for Negro League teams.

Greenberg supported Robinson from the start. "The more they ride him the more they will spur him on. It threw me a lot when I first came up. I know how he feels," Greenberg told a reporter.

Besides the twenty-five homers he hit for Pittsburgh, Greenberg's greatest contribution to his new team during the 1947 season was, as he described it, training his "own successor," Ralph Kiner.

Kiner, an outfielder, recalled that when he first met Greenberg, Kiner did not like what he heard: "'Kid,'" Greenberg said, "'I don't think you're going to ever be a great home run hitter.' I thought he was kidding me," Kiner said, "'cause I had led the league in home runs the year before in the National League." Kiner kept listening, though. "'I think you stand too far from the plate in the batter's box,'" Greenberg told the young player. "'And to be a home run hitter, you have to pull the ball.'" After their first conversation, the two players spent hours together perfecting Kiner's swing. "I think one of the most important things I learned about that, you're not going to change overnight ... It's going to take a lot of hard work," Kiner added.

Greenberg believed in Kiner. "He had a natural home-run swing," said Greenberg. "All he needed was somebody to teach him the value of hard work and self-discipline."

As he said he would, Greenberg retired at the end of the season. Although his one season with the Pirates was not spectacular, he played well and was responsible for the highest ticket sales in the team's history. "Hank Greenberg's drawing power at the gate [was] a vital factor in compiling these extraordinary statistics," reported the *New York Times*. Team owner John Galbreath, grateful for Greenberg's contributions, wrote Greenberg a letter at the end of the season. "You fulfilled every promise you made," he wrote. "No one could have tried any harder or given any more time and effort to try to earnestly carry out every letter of a contract than you did."

Right before his retirement, he attended the 1947 World Series between the Brooklyn Dodgers and the New York Yankees. There he met Bill Veeck, the principal owner and president of the Cleveland Indians. The two men got along well and met several times before Veeck invited Greenberg to join the Indians' organization. Veeck did not have a specific job in mind for Greenberg, but he did want to teach the former slugger about life in the front office, and Greenberg was a willing student.

Jackie Robinson was the first African American to play Major League Baseball. He played second base for the Brooklyn Dodgers from 1947 to 1956.

At the beginning of the 1948 season, rather than putting on his uniform and running out to first base, Greenberg now wore a suit and tie and began learning the business of baseball. "Veeck converted me. I was a ballplayer, you see, and the game was everything … Bill taught me that baseball was more than just balls and strikes, hits and errors. You have to get people into the ball park, and to do that you have to attract them with a good time as well as a good team."

After a few months, Greenberg was named the director of the Indians' farm system.

Following the birth of son Stephen in September of 1948, the Greenbergs were now a family of four. They settled in a suburb of Cleveland, and Caral became involved with Cleveland's horse-riding community. "I had show horses, but Hank wasn't too interested in them," she said. Caral was never really happy in Cleveland, and her husband's long hours at the office did not help her adjust to life away from family and friends. "There were a lot of activities on weekends," Caral said about her involvement in Cleveland's cultural and horse-riding events. "I went out all the time. Hank was always at the ballpark on weekends."

In 1949, Bill Veeck sold the Indians to a new owner, Ellis Ryan, who asked Greenberg to become the team's general manager and take responsibility for acquiring new players and managing their contracts.

Greenberg's promotion put new kinds of pressure on the two-time MVP. Not surprisingly, Greenberg felt most confident in dealing with the players themselves. "I'm fair with the ballplayers because I am naturally sympathetic to them," he said. "On the other hand, I'm difficult in that I demand that they put out. I remember the way I felt when I was a player about certain men on the ball club who weren't putting out all they might have."

During his time in Cleveland, Greenberg received a letter from a Jewish doctor in Philadelphia asking for advice for a young Jewish baseball player. "Baseball is a game that affords any youngster an opportunity to progress," he replied. "Ability is the sole determining factor in advancement, and not

After retiring as an active player, Greenberg moved to the administrative side of baseball. He was the director of the Cleveland Indians' farm system before becoming their general manager. Later, he owned a small percentage of the baseball club.

religion, the way your hair parts or your parental lineage." In a hand-written postscript, he added: "If prejudice does exist and I refuse to recognize that it does, then let it spur you on to greater achievement rather than accept it and be licked by it."

Greenberg's own experience with prejudice motivated him to improve life on the road for some of his players. While traveling with the Indians in 1955, Greenberg noticed that when the bus arrived at a hotel in Baltimore, the Indians' five black players remained seated. "What do you guys do?" he asked them. "'We wait for a taxi, and this taxi takes us to different homes, different families in Baltimore, and we stay with them,'" one of the players told him.

Greenberg understood how it felt to be an outsider, and he made his feelings clear. "Here these fellows are a vital part of the team and contributing greatly to the success of the team, and they have to be segregated." The black players were not separated for long. After learning that hotels in St. Louis, Baltimore, and Washington, D.C., did not permit blacks to stay with the rest of the team, Greenberg instructed the Indians' traveling coordinator to send letters to the hotels stating that they would "have to take all of our players; it was that or none at all." Until he journeyed with the team, he was unaware of how the players were being treated.

Although Greenberg was able to improve conditions for some of his players, there continued to be too many empty seats in the Cleveland stands. The team owners were also frustrated about four second-place finishes to the Yankees. Arthur Daley wrote in the *New York Times* that the former slugger was "a victim of circumstance." "Once the fans begin to second-guess a guy, he can't win," Daley wrote, and "Hank was second-guessed to a fare-thee-well."

Making things more complicated was that the Greenbergs, now the parents of three children (a daughter, Alva, was born in 1952), decided to divorce. "While she liked baseball, she wasn't the type of wife who came to every game and followed every box score," Greenberg said of Caral. "She had other interests, and sometimes our two worlds seemed to grow further apart."

The Greenbergs were granted joint custody of their two sons and young daughter. After Caral returned to New York City, Greenberg also rented an apartment there so that the children could be near both parents.

In 1956, Greenberg learned that he and Joe Cronin, former Red Sox shortstop, had been elected to the National Baseball Hall of Fame. Greenberg later said that when the phone call came, he "thought about the hours I had spent on the ball field and now how every single bit of effort I put into improving myself as a player was worth it." In July, he and Joe Cronin were enshrined in Cooperstown, New York.

Greenberg stands with Joe Cronin, former Boston Red Sox shortstop, during their induction to the National Baseball Hall of Fame in 1956. Greenberg was the first Jewish player to be inducted into baseball's shrine.

Elected by members of the Baseball Writers' Association of America, the members of the Hall of Fame are a select group.

"These were the true immortals, demi-gods of such enormous skills that their fabled feats assumed an almost legendary grandeur," sports columnist Arthur Daley wrote in his *New York Times* article about Greenberg and Cronin.

In the speech he made during the induction ceremony, with his brothers, Joe and Ben, and his sister, Lillian, looking on, Greenberg said: "In all my years of being on the playing field, I never dreamed that this would be the

Greenberg (center) with two baseball greats, Roger Maris (left) and Joe DiMaggio. Maris surpassed Babe Ruth's home run record by hitting sixty-one home runs for the New York Yankees during the 1961 season. DiMaggio spent thirteen years with the New York Yankees and in 1941 had a fifty-six-consecutive-game hitting streak.

final result. I can't possibly express how I feel. It's just too wonderful for words. I'm deeply grateful and humble for this great honor."

After two more years, he was released from the Indians organization in 1958. But there was another opportunity waiting in Chicago. Greenberg, along with his old friend Bill Veeck, bought an interest in the Chicago White Sox, and he began traveling to Chicago regularly. "I was involved in running a ball club in Chicago and a family in New York," he said. "It was quite an adjustment."

In 1959, he accepted an offer to become vice president and part owner of the Chicago White Sox, making Greenberg the first Jewish co-owner of a Major League Baseball team. While he enjoyed the challenges of owning a baseball team, traveling between New York and Chicago was difficult. "I felt I couldn't run the club on a day-to-day basis because I had children in New York and I planned to live there permanently. So we parted on very friendly terms," he said. Greenberg stayed in Chicago for only two years before returning to New York and pursuing a career in finance.

Years before joining the White Sox organization, Greenberg had met Mary Jo DeCicco, a former actress. At the time of their first meeting, both were married, but by 1961, each of them had gone through a divorce, and they began dating. Although DeCicco lived across the country, Greenberg wanted to stay in New York with his three children. "I would fly out to California at least three or four times a year, and she would come to New York once a year," Greenberg later recalled. "We kept this up until we finally got married in 1966."

They settled in New York and spent summers in California. Over the years, however, Mary Jo continued to miss living in California. After Greenberg's two sons were married and his daughter was studying at Kenyon College in Ohio, they decided to move. In 1974, the couple bought a house in Beverly Hills. Soon after joining the Beverly Hills Tennis Club, Greenberg began to spend more time playing tennis, a sport he had enjoyed during his years in Cleveland.

By 1974, Greenberg had turned his athletic attention from baseball to tennis. He excelled as a tennis player on the senior circuit.

He quickly became a regular in celebrity tennis tournaments and was so recognizable as a tennis player that one day, after signing an autograph at a tournament, a woman whispered to her son, "That's Hank Greenberg, the tennis star."

In the fall of 1985, seventy-four-year-old Greenberg learned he had kidney cancer. After surgery, during which doctors removed one of his kidneys, Greenberg was optimistic about his chances to survive. "I think there was that part of my dad that really felt he was invincible," his son Stephen said. "I can remember now how, when I was a little kid, he used to talk to me about the importance of physical exercise, building up your body, playing different sports … so when he was faced with cancer he couldn't believe it. He couldn't believe his body had let him down."

Greenberg underwent radiation and surgery and felt strong enough that he and Mary Jo hosted their annual New Year's Eve party. But by the summer of 1986, Greenberg was not feeling well and returned to the hospital for more radiation treatments. "I have my fingers crossed that this might be the solution to my problem," he said.

Hammerin' Hank remained hopeful, but it was soon clear that his condition was deteriorating and more radiation would not cure him.

At the end of the summer, on September 4, 1986, during an exhibition game between the Mets and the Red Sox, Ralph Kiner, the former Pittsburgh Pirate and now a broadcaster, was handed a press release. "This is the worst day of my life," Kiner said into the microphone. "My dearest friend, and the man who was like a father to me, Hank Greenberg, has died."

During his thirteen-year career, Hammerin' Hank Greenberg became one of baseball's greatest hitters and a hero to Jews in America.

12

HAMMERIN' HANK'S LEGACY

SOME BASEBALL PLAYERS CONTINUE TO inspire people long after their careers are over. Hank Greenberg is one of them—not only because he was the first Jewish baseball star or because of the 1938 season when he came within two home runs of breaking Babe Ruth's record, but because of the way he conducted himself, both on and off the field.

After his death in 1986, an editorial in the *Detroit News* read: "He gave selflessly to any number of individuals and causes, without issuing self-aggrandizing press releases. If you don't believe that, just watch. Praise will flow from places you never considered: from entertainers, politicians, tennis players, celebrities, groundskeepers, restaurant owners, sportswriters, baseball fans."

The editorial's author was right. Praise and stories came from everywhere.

Jewish actor Walter Matthau grew up on New York's Lower East Side and was one of Greenberg's fans. Remembering the six-foot-four, 210-pound Jewish star, Matthau said, "You couldn't help but be exhilarated by the sight of one of our own guys looking like Colossus," referring to a giant statue, one of the Seven Wonders of the Ancient World. He "was part of my dreams, part of my aspirations. I wanted to be Hank Greenberg."

Alan Dershowitz, a prominent Jewish lawyer, told a filmmaker that as a kid, he thought Hank Greenberg would "become the first Jewish president."

Bud Shaver of the *Detroit Times* recalled Greenberg showing him a letter from a thirteen-year-old Jewish girl. The teenager's letter expressed her disappointment that Max Baer, a Jewish boxer, had lost the heavyweight championship in 1935. She was now "banking all on Hank … and begged him not to fail her or his people." Shaver wrote that when he gave the letter back to Greenberg, he told him: "'You have an immense responsibility.' Hank's face was grave as he tucked the soiled little letter away in his pocket. 'Yes I have,' he said soberly." "To that little girl," Shaver wrote, "Hank is a Jew in shining armor."

Harry Eisenstat, a Jewish pitcher, said, "I saw him once after a game with some ballplayer … and a kid went over to the player and asked for an autograph. The player had lost the game the day before and he was nasty to the kid and refused to sign his autograph. The kid felt shunned … Hank went over to the kid, the kid was in tears, sent for a ball, signed it and gave it to him."

Al Rosen, another Jewish baseball player, said, "Greenberg was really a pathfinder, accomplishing much like what Jackie Robinson did for blacks in baseball ... Hank paved the way for people like me."

One of Greenberg's friends recalled an incident that helps explain Greenberg's character. "In those years, there was a little crippled kid who sold pencils outside the Leland [Hotel]. Worse case of paralysis I ever saw. His face was all twisted, I never understood a word he said. But Hank was always doing things for that kid. He'd have him up for dinner in his [Greenberg's] suite or the dining room. It was as if he saw something in him, something that might have been if he hadn't had such a bad break in life."

Another friend remembered that "Hank was one of the first to charge for his autograph, but the checks were made out to Pets Adoption, his favorite charity. Only a few of us knew that Hank matched every dollar sent in out of his own pocket."

Talking with a writer near the end of his life, Greenberg said, "It's a strange thing. When I was playing, I used to resent being singled out as a Jewish ballplayer. I wanted to be known as a great ballplayer, period. I'm not sure why or when I changed, because I'm still not a particularly religious person. Lately, though, I find myself wanting to be remembered not only as a great ballplayer, but even more as a great Jewish ballplayer."

HANK GREENBERG NAMES HIS OWN ALL-STAR BASEBALL TEAM

FIRST BASE

Lou Gehrig—New York Yankees

Lou Gehrig, nicknamed "The Iron Horse" for playing 2,130 consecutive games, died tragically at the age of thirty-seven of amyotrophic lateral sclerosis (ALS) disease. ALS is now commonly referred to as Lou Gehrig's disease.

SECOND BASE

Charlie Gehringer—Detroit Tigers

Greenberg's teammate played for the Tigers between 1924 and 1942 and batted over .300 for thirteen seasons.

THIRD BASE

Harold "Pie" Traynor—Pittsburgh Pirates

A .320 career hitter, Pie Traynor was the star of the Pirates between 1920 and 1935.

SHORTSTOP

Honus Wagner—Pittsburgh Pirates

Honus Wagner, the shortstop for the Pittsburgh Pirates between 1900 and 1917, was one of the five original inductees to the Baseball Hall of Fame in 1936.

OUTFIELD

Ty Cobb—Detroit Tigers

Nicknamed "The Georgia Peach," Cobb was known as a fierce competitor and a great hitter, batting over .300 for twenty-three consecutive seasons.

OUTFIELD
Babe Ruth—New York Yankees

George Herman "Babe" Ruth played in the American League between 1914 and 1934. His lifetime total of 714 home runs was the record for thirty-nine years, until it was broken by Hank Aaron in 1974.

OUTFIELD
Joe DiMaggio—New York Yankees

A longtime player for the Yankees, DiMaggio is best remembered for his fifty-six-consecutive-game hitting streak in 1941.

CATCHER
Mickey Cochrane—Philadelphia Athletics and Detroit Tigers

Another of Greenberg's teammates, Cochrane was known for his competitive spirit both on and off the field. He batted .320 during his thirteen-year career.

PITCHER
Robert "Lefty" Grove—Philadelphia Athletics and Boston Red Sox

Lefty Grove was the premier player for the Philadelphia Athletics between 1929 and 1931, during which time the team record was an amazing 79–15.

PITCHER
Bob Feller—Cleveland Indians

A right-handed fastball pitcher for the Indians for eighteen seasons, Feller compiled 266 wins and had 2,581 strikeouts.

FURTHER RESOURCES

If you want to learn more about Hank Greenberg:

Watch
The Life and Times of Hank Greenberg, a film by Aviva Kempner, 1998

Baseball: A Film by Ken Burns
www.pbs.org/kenburns/baseball*

Visit
National Baseball Hall of Fame
Cooperstown, New York (1-888-HALL-OF-FAME)
www.baseballhalloffame.org

Comerica Park, home of the Detroit Tigers. Six of the Tigers' greatest players are honored at Comerica Park with statues located along the left center-field wall. The thirteen-foot high sculptures pay tribute to the contributions of Hank Greenberg, Ty Cobb, Charlie Gehringer, Willie Horton, Al Kaline, and Hal Newhouser.

International Tennis Hall of Fame
194 Bellevue Avenue
Newport, Rhode Island 02840
www.tennisfame.com

Read
Hammerin' Hank: The Life of Hank Greenberg by Yona Zeldis McDonough
Walker Books for Young Readers, 2006

Hank Greenberg: Hall-of-Fame Slugger by Ira Berkow
Jewish Publication Society of America, 2001

Hank Greenberg: The Story of My Life by Hank Greenberg with Ira Berkow
Triumph Books, 2001

Web sites active at time of publication

To read more about the history of the times when Hank Greenberg played baseball:

Children of the Great Depression by Russell Freedman
Clarion Books, 2005

Dear Mrs. Roosevelt: Letters from Children of the Great Depression
edited by Robert Cohen
University of North Carolina Press, 2007

FDR's Alphabet Soup: New Deal America, 1932–1939 by Tonya Bolden
Knopf Books for Young Readers, 2010

Franklin Delano Roosevelt by Russell Freedman
Clarion Books, 1992

The Good Fight: How World War II Was Won by Stephen E. Ambrose
Atheneum, 2001

Hitler Youth: Growing Up in Hitler's Shadow by Susan Campbell Bartoletti
Scholastic, 2005

Knockout! A Photobiography of Boxer Joe Louis by George Sullivan
National Geographic Children's Books, 2008

The Life and Death of Adolf Hitler by James Cross Giblin
Clarion Books, 2002

The Nazi Olympics: Berlin 1936 by Susan D. Bachrach
Little, Brown, 2000

BIBLIOGRAPHY

Alexander, Charles C. *Breaking the Slump: Baseball in the Depression Era*. New York: Columbia University Press, 2002.

Angell, Roger. *Let Me Finish*. Orlando, FL: Harcourt, 2006.

Bachrach, Susan D. *The Nazi Olympics: Berlin 1936*. Boston: Little, Brown, 2000.

Bak, Richard. *Cobb Would Have Caught It: The Golden Age of Baseball in Detroit*. Detroit: Wayne State University Press, 1991.

———. *Joe Louis: The Great Black Hope*. Dallas: Da Capo Press, 1996.

The Detroit News. Home, Sweet Home: Memories of Tiger Stadium. Detroit: Sports Publishing Inc., 1999.

Dreifort, John E., ed. *Baseball History from Outside the Lines*. Lincoln: University of Nebraska Press, 2001.

Eig, Jonathan. *Luckiest Man: The Life and Death of Lou Gehrig*. New York: Simon and Schuster, 2005.

Falls, Joe. *The Detroit Tigers: An Illustrated History*. New York: Prentice Hall, 1989.

Fitzgerald, Ed. "Hank Greenberg: A Study in Success." *Sport*, March 1951.

Gavrilovich, Peter, and Bill McPraw, eds. *The Detroit Almanac: 300 Years of Life in the Motor City*. Detroit: Detroit Free Press, 2000.

Greenberg, Hank. *Hank Greenberg, The Story of My Life*. Edited and with an introduction by Ira Berkow. Chicago: Triumph Books, 2001.

Hill, Art. *I Don't Care If I Never Come Back: A Baseball Fan and His Game*. New York: Simon and Schuster, 1980.

James, Bill. *The New Bill James Historical Baseball Abstract*. New York: Free Press, 2001.

Jeansonne, Glen. *Women of the Far Right: The Mothers' Movement and World War II*. Chicago: University of Chicago Press, 1997.

Kennedy, David M. *Freedom from Fear: The American People in Depression and War, 1929–1945*. New York: Oxford University Press, 2005.

Levine, Peter. *Ellis Island to Ebbets Field: Sport and the American Jewish Experience*. New York: Oxford University Press, 1992.

Marzejka, Laurie J. "The Tigers' Hammerin' Hank Greenberg." *Detroit News* (accessed April 28, 2004).

McCollister, John. *The Tigers and Their Den: The Official Story of the Detroit Tigers.* Lenexa, KS: Addax Publishing, 1999.

McDonough, Yona Zeldis. *Hammerin' Hank: The Life of Hank Greenberg.* New York: Walker Books for Young Readers, 2006.

Myler, Patrick. *Ring of Hate: Joe Louis v Max Schmeling and the Bitter Propaganda War.* Edinburgh, IN: Mainstream Publishing, 2005.

Povich, Shirley. *All Those Mornings ... At the* Post: *The 20th Century in Sports from Famed* Washington Post *Columnist Shirley Povich.* New York: Public Affairs, 2005.

Ritter, Lawrence S. *The Glory of Their Times: The Story of the Early Days of Baseball Told by the Men Who Played It.* New York: Harper Perennial, 2002.

Simons, William M. *The Cooperstown Symposium on Baseball and American Culture, 2002.* Jefferson, NC: McFarland, 2003.

Ultan, Lloyd. *The Beautiful Bronx: 1920–1950.* New York: Harmony Books, 1979.

Vincent, Fay. *The Only Game in Town: Baseball Stars of the 1930s and 1940s Talk About the Game They Loved.* New York: Simon and Schuster, 2006.

Wallace, Joseph E. *The Autobiography of Baseball: The Inside Story from the Stars Who Played the Game.* New York: Harry N. Abrams, 1998.

Warren, Donald. *Radio Priest: Charles Coughlin, the Father of Hate Radio.* New York: Free Press, 1996.

DVDs

The Life and Times of Hank Greenberg. A Film by Aviva Kempner. The Ciesla Foundation, 1998.

New York. Directed by Ric Burns. PBS Paramount, 1999.

SOURCE NOTES

The source of each quotation in this book is found below. The citation indicates the first words of the quotation and its document source. The sources are listed in the bibliography.

The following abbreviations are used:

HG *(Hank Greenberg: The Story of My Life* by Hank Greenberg with Ira Berkow)
HOF (National Baseball Hall of Fame, Hank Greenberg File)
GTT *(The Glory of Their Times* by Lawrence S. Ritter)

Chapter One   page 8

"Hey, coal mine …": HG, p. 181.
"I forgot to ask you …": same as above.
"Class tells …": same as above.
"Kike …": HG, p. 40.
"Jew bastard …": same as above, p. 50.
"Young man, I just came from …": same as above, p. 11.
"I began to think …": GTT, p. 309.
"Jewish ballplayer …": HG, p. xii.
"In the case of Jackie Robinson …": same as above, p. 98.
"There was nobody…": same as above.
"Must the entire world …": detnews.com/Michigan History, July 23, 1995.
      (also on page 33 of *Women of the Far Right: The Mothers' Movement and World War II* by Glen Jeansonne).
"Schmeling's victory …": Bachrach, p. 60.

Chapter Two   page 14

"anytime there was less …": HG, p. 1.
"largest Jewish city …": *New York*/Burns.
"I thought I was in Heaven …": same as above.
"He kept the house …": HG, p. 5.
"A small group of …": same as above, p. 4.
"Kids down in the village …": same as above.
"a turning point …": same as above, p. 5.
"to prove that I wasn't …": HG, p. 8.
"awkward …": GTT, p. 309.
"At school, I'd squeeze …": same as above.
"hours on end …": HG, p. 1.
"On weekdays after school …": same as above.
"My father used to holler at me …": same as above, p. 3.
"It was like …": same as above, p. 6.
"Travel was restricted …": same as above.
"I still remember …": GTT, p. 308.

"The lights would flash ...": HG, p. 6.
"In those days ...": Ultan, p. 34.
"You do this all day long ...": GTT, p. 309.
"In basketball, I was much taller ...": HG, p. 12.
"Look up the record.": HOF.

Chapter Three   page 24

"Wherever I played ...": GTT, p. 310.
"I am an amateur" and the rest of Lippe story through "Ten dollars ...": HG, p. 13.
Information on New York Yankees looking for Jewish player: Eig, p. 133.
"How'd you like ...": HG, p. 16.
"His shoulders were ...": GTT, p. 310.
"I had a look at ...": Eig, p. 133.
"They figured that if ...": *Sport,* March 1951, HOF.
"Pop, I've got to go ...": HG, p. 18.
"I just sat around ...": same as above, p. 20.
"did not want to mingle ...": same as above, p. 20.
"Playing semipro ball ...": same as above, p. 21.
"Because I was a first baseman ...": same as above.
"a total bust..." same as above, p. 21.
"My teammates were ...": same as above, p. 22.
"hollered the full length ...": same as above, p. 21.
"It wasn't hard to talk ...": same as above, p. 22.
"I was as good ...": same as above, p. 24.
"looked at my driver's license ...": same as above, p. 25.
"As a rule, Jewish boys ...": "Oi, Oi, Oh Boy! Hail That Long-Sought Hebrew Star" by
     Frederick G. Lieb, *Sporting News*, September 12, 1935, HOF.
"If you can make the grade ...": HG, p. 26.
"All my hard work ...": same as above, p. 27.
"Hot as blazes" through "... hundred degrees.": same as above, p. 30.

Chapter Four   page 34

Information on tickets as luxury: Falls, p. 70.
"Attending a game ...": Angell, p. 65.
"Everybody dressed ...": Falls, p. 67.
"sailing their hats": *Detroit News,* p. 90.
"I knew things were tough ...": Falls, p. 70.
"Most everyone was broke ...": GTT, p. 313.
"When I first came ...": Falls, p. 73.
General information on Detroit: Alexander, p. 1.
"I put on a fielder's glove ...": HG, p. 36.
"big sweaty kid ...": same as above.
Meeting with Navin: GTT, p. 313.
"big, awkward ...": HG, p. 306.

Chapter Five page 42

"My first year in Detroit …": HG, p. 41.
Information on Joe Muer's Fish House: Falls, p. 74.
"become the first …": *The Life and Times of Hank Greenberg*/Kempner.
"Many times I'd go into …": HG, p. 75.
"There was a big …" through "Napoleon of the Bronx!": same as above, p. 44.
"I don't think anybody …": Alexander, p. 92.
"Jewish Babe Ruth": Bak, *Cobb*, p. 56.
Babe Ruth statistics: National Baseball Hall of Fame.
"the Jewish ballplayer": HG, p. xii.
"They always had …": Falls, p. 74.
"I could take it …": Falls, p.74.
"sidled up to the player in question …": Levine, p. 139.
"Listen, we're going to win …": HG, p. 49.
"Hank, of course …": Bak, *Cobb*, p. 201.
"Just about every morning …": same as above, p. 362.
"Henry Greenberg dealt …": HG, p. 52.
"The development of Greenberg …": same as above, p. 53.
"became a national issue …": GTT, p. 330.
"We are an Orthodox family …": HG, p. 57.
"I didn't know what …": same as above, p. 55.
"He consulted the Talmud …": GTT, p. 330.
"I hit two home runs …": same as above.
"everything seemed to stop …" and rest of synagogue story: Bak, *Cobb*, p. 56.
"the greatest player the Jews …": Levine, p. 135.
"in position to do …": same as above, pp. 135–136.
"The Irish didn't like it …": GTT, p. 331.
"I was a hero …": HG, p. 58.

Chapter Six page 50

Information about Gashouse Gang: McCollister, p. 82.
"so nervous …": HG, p. 65.
"We had to start …": same as above, p. 66.
"I'm happy for …": McCollister, p. 85.
"The Cardinals gave …": HG, p. 67.
"the ablest Jew in baseball …": *New Yorker* magazine, October 6, 1934.
Conversation with Navin: Falls, p. 75.
"No way was I going …": same as above.
"In 1935, that $15,000 …": HG, p. 71.
"I notice in the papers …": same as above, p. 68.
Information on Joe Roggin: Bak, *Cobb*, p. 72.
"Hank would come over …": same as above.
"… they started riding me …": HG, p. 78.
"Throw him a pork chop …": same as above.

"I slid into home plate …" through "… snapped it back.": same as above, p. 80.
"hear the sound …": McCollister, p. 87.
"a keen blow …": HG, p. 81.
"This is the greatest day …": McCollister, p. 89.

Chapter Seven   page 58

Information on Detroit sports teams: McCollister, p. 91.
"They put a heavy weight …": Bak, *Joe Louis*, p. 90.
"toast of Harlem": same as above, p. 91.
Information on Hitler: Kennedy, p. 383.
"Radio Priest": Levine, p. 135.
"a powerful minority …": Warren, p. 155.
"For the first and only time …" through "… among the missing.": HG, p. 84.
"Greenberg's fight for more dough …": HOF.
"My response was that …": HG, p. 85.
"All I was trying …": same as above.
Information on 1936 Olympics: Bachrach, pp. 49, 70.
"most humiliating …": same as above, p. 103.

Chapter Eight   page 66

"I was full of confidence …": HG, p. 89.
"If we had a man on …": GTT, p. 316.
"With him [York] behind me …": HG, p. 91.
"lost sight of the ball …": Bak, *Cobb,* p. 78.
"crashed into his …": same as above.
"fame and credit …": Levine, p. 137.
"all the Jewish boys …" through "… leadership of boys.": same as above.
"On real good ball clubs …": Vincent, p. 73.
"the Nazi party's darling …": Myler, p. 99.
"I know you won it …": same as above.
"beat the Negro …": Myler, p. 99.
"We need muscles …": same as above, p. 133.
"Joe Louis Knocked Out Hitler": Bak, *Joe Louis*, p. 167.
"The strain is too great …": HG, p. 105.
"I knew he was under …": same as above, p. 106.
"He walks up and down …": same as above.
"was close to tears …": same as above, p. 103.
"I've heard that question …": same as above, p. 104.
"Greenberg, reported the Associated Press …": same as above, p. 108.
"He always kept …": same as above, p. 109.
Gefilte fish story: Levine, p. 139.
"There is no shuffle …": HG, p. 109.
"They could deny Jewish boys …": Simons, p. 93.
"Being Jewish did carry …": Bak, *Cobb*, p. 85.

"In Europe, they are asking ...": HG, p. 111.
Pitchers' quotes: same as above, p. 110.
"the greatest game of his life ...": same as above, p. 112.
"so mad that he kicked ...": same as above, p. 112.
Quotes from Feller paragraph: same as above, p. 113.
"It kept getting darker ...": same as above, pp. 113–114.
"I'm sorry, Hank ...": same as above.
"That's all right, George ...": *Chicago Daily News*, July 27, 1961, HOF.

Chapter Nine   page 76

"First of all ..." through "I was satisfied...": "How to Hit a Home Run" by Hank Greenberg.
    Collier's, April 22, 1939, HOF.
"I don't think ..." through "He was one of us.": HG, p. 111.
Story about George McQuinn who dropped ball: Bak, *Cobb*, p. 85.
"We used to go down ...": HG, p. 116.
"an enormously impressive figure ...": *Sport*, March 1951, HOF.
"I was young ...": HG, p. 116.
"Hank has been connected ...": *Sport*, p. 135, HOF.
"married to some nice ...": *Sporting News*, November 7, 1940, HOF.
"I rarely went out ...": HG, p. 126.
Information on Lou Gehrig: same as above, pp. 119–120.
"While I didn't have ...": same as above, pp. 120–121.
Quotes and information about moving to outfield: same as above, p. 121.
"I was strong. ...": same as above, p. 122.
McCosky and new suit story: same as above, p. 123.
"I used to see Joe ...": HG, p. 88.
"You have to ...": same as above, p. 124.
"Hank did something ...": same as above, p. 129.
Information on first year in outfield: McCollister, p. 96.
"a lot easier ...": GTT, p. 321.
"I didn't have to take ...": same as above.
"It's like a Broadway traffic cop ...": HG, p. 128.
"I can't say that ...": same as above, p. 125.
"Gehringer is probably ..." through "There's no antidote ...": same as above, p. 134.
"What a disappointed ...": same as above, p. 135.

Chapter Ten   page 86

"What's all the fuss ...": HG, p. 137.
"I was thirty years old ...": same as above, p. 140.
"To my mind ...": same as above, p. 139.
"Through it all ...": *Sport*, March 1951, HOF.
Prison story with quotes: GTT, p. 324.
"I got a big hand ...": HG, p. 141.
"I headed back ...": same as above.

"Baseball is out …": same as above, p. 142.
"But all the time …": Levine, p. 141.
"I had my fill …": HG, p. 142.
"I'll never forget … clock-like precision …": same as above, p. 143.
"saw he wasn't …": same as above.
Number of professional baseball players in military service: Alexander, p. 280.
"I honestly feel that …": Bak, *Cobb*, p. 110.
Information on "The Star-Spangled Banner": same as above, p. 111.
Information on Detroit manufacturing: McCollister, p. 105.
"At the moment Detroit …": HG, pp. 129–130.
"Nobody has ever …": same as above, p. 145.
"A Great Soldier, A Great Ball Player …": HOF.
Wheaties box quote: Levine, p. 142.
"Everybody was cheering …": HG, p. 146.
"I wasn't sure whether …": Bak, *Cobb*, p. 122.
"When we returned …": HG, p. 148.
"I had been in the service …": same as above, p. 149.
"He said, 'You don't have to feel …'": same as above, p. 152.
"I had no knowledge …": same as above, p. 153.
"We searched out …": same as above, pp. 153–154.

Chapter Eleven   page 98

Information about Detroit girls wearing black socks: McCollister, p. 116.
"I had seen a lot of things …": HG, p. 157.
"agile or quick …": same as above, p. 158.
"The years had taken …": same as above, p. 160.
"He did not look so good …": same as above, p. 164.
"This is to inform you …": same as above, p. 169.
"Greenberg Big Favorite" and quotes: HOF.
"I don't want to talk …": GTT, p. 325.
"If I ever did play …": same as above, pp. 325–326.
"Baseball was still …": HG, p. 173.
"The more they ride him …": same as above, p. 181.
Kiner quotes: Vincent, p. 203.
"He had a natural …": GTT, p. 326.
"Hank Greenberg's drawing power …": HG, p. 187.
"You fulfilled every promise …": same as above, p. 187.
"Veeck converted me …": GTT, p. 328.
"I had show horses …": HG, p. 219.
"I'm fair with the ballplayers …" *Sport*, March 1951, HOF.
"Baseball is a game that affords …": HOF.
"What do you guys do …" through the rest of the story: HG, pp. 209–210.
"A victim of circumstance" through "…fare-thee-well.": *New York Times*, October 22, 1957,
    HOF.
"While she liked baseball …": HG, p. 217.

"thought about the hours …": *Sporting News*, February 8, 1956, HOF.

"These were the true immortals …": *New York Times*, January 30, 1956, HOF.

"In all my years of being …": *Washington Post*, September 5, 1986, HOF.

"I was involved in running …": HG, p. 218.

"I felt I couldn't run …": same as above, p. 236.

"I would fly out …": same as above, p. 247.

"That's Hank Greenberg, the tennis star.": HOF.

"I think there was …": HG, pp. 262–263.

"I have my fingers crossed …": same as above, p. 268.

"This is the worst day …": same as above, p. 268.

Chapter Twelve   page 112

"He gave selflessly …": *Detroit News*. detnews.com/history/Greenberg (accessed April 28, 2004).

"You couldn't help …": *The Life and Times of Hank Greenberg*/Kempner.

"become the first …": same as above.

Max Baer story (with quotes): Levine, p. 137.

Eisenstat's story about the autograph: HG, p. 100.

"Greenberg was really …": Levine, p. 140.

"In those years ...": *Detroit News*. detnews.com/history/Greenberg (accessed April 28, 2004).

"Hank was one of the first …": *Detroit News*. detnews.com/history/Greenberg (accessed April 28, 2004).

"It's a strange thing …": *Newsday*, September 28, 1986, HOF.

INDEX

Page numbers in *italics* refer to photographs and/or captions.

CREDITS

Picture Credits

AP Images, AP/WIDE WORLD PHOTOS: 11, 56, 68, 72, 83, 93, 98, 103.

Detroit News/Home, Sweet Home, from the Collection of the *Detroit News*: 34, 36–37.

The Granger Collection, New York: 18, 22, 32–33, 52, 58, 60, 62, 64, 70.

The John F. Kennedy Presidential Library and Museum, Boston: 100.

Library of Congress, Prints and Photographs Division: LC-USZ62-107837: 16; LC-USZ62-845: 21; LC-DIG-ppmsca-15308: 24; LC-B2-2210-2: 26; LC-USZ62-97880: 28; LC-B2-3225-7: 29; LC-USZ62-27663: 65; LC-DIG-ppmsca-19857: 91.

National Baseball Hall of Fame & Museum, Cooperstown, New York: BL-5113.7b (copyright status undetermined): front cover, page 3; BL-801.78: front and back cover, 57, endpapers; BL-2828.82: 8, 112; BL-20.48: 12, 96; BL-929.93 (copyright status undetermined): 14; BL-4737.89, Frank Osheowitz: 19; BL-3131.83: 23; BL-13388.95 (copyright status undetermined): 39; BL-1048.91: 42; BL-127.98, R. G. Hank Utley (copyright status undetermined): 44–45; BL-815.68: 50; BL-1491.68WT: 66; BL-229.85 (copyright status undetermined): 76; BL-3408.63: 79; BL-510.68: 80; BL-1233.98, David Barrett (copyright status undetermined): 81; BL-2466.70 (copyright status undetermined): 84; BL-723.63 (copyright status undetermined): 86; BL-3932.76: 88; BL-723.63 (copyright status undetermined): 89; BL-5915.91, © Bettmann/CORBIS, Doug Walker: 94; BL-1491.68WT: 97; BL-4920.70 (copyright status undetermined): 105; BL-4221.71 (copyright status undetermined): 107; photo by William Greene (copyright status undetermined): 108; BL-1716.77 (copyright status undetermined): 110.

Text Credits

Excerpts from *Hank Greenberg, The Story of My Life* by Hank Greenberg, edited and with an introduction by Ira Berkow; used with permission.